living
BEYOND MY
CIRCUMSTANCES

Deborah L. Willows
with Steph Beth Nickel

Foreword by Joni Eareckson Tada

CASTLE QUAY BOOKS
WWW.CASTLEQUAYBOOKS.COM

Living Beyond My Circumstances: The Deborah Willows Story

International Standard Book Number: 978-1-927355-18-3
ISBN 978-1-927355-17-6 EPUB

Published by:
Castle Quay Books
Pickering, Ontario
Tel: (416) 573-3249
E-mail: info@castlequaybooks.com   www.castlequaybooks.com

Edited by Marina Hofman Willard
Cover design by Burst Impressions

Some names have been changed.
Front cover photo and photo on page 48 were taken by *London Free Press*.

Printed at Essence Publishing, Belleville, Ontario

Library and Archives Canada Cataloguing in Publication
Willows, Deborah, 1961-, author
Living beyond my circumstances : the Deborah Willows
story / Deborah Willows with Steph Beth Nickel ; foreword by
Joni Eareckson Tada ; note from the Honourable David C. Onley.

Includes bibliographical references.
Issued in print and electronic formats.
ISBN 978-1-927355-18-3 (pbk.).—ISBN 978-1-927355-17-6 (epub)

1. Willows, Deborah, 1961- —Health. 2. Cerebral palsied—Canada—
Biography. 3. People with disabilities—Canada—Biography. 4. Olympic
athletes—Canada—Biography. I. Nickel, Steph Beth, 1961-, author II. Title.

RC388.W54 2013   362.19892'8360092   C2013-907943-2
                                                                          C2013-907944-0

CASTLE QUAY BOOKS
WWW.CASTLEQUAYBOOKS.COM

Dedication

This book is dedicated to Jesus Christ, my Saviour and Lord. Without Him, my life and this book would be meaningless.

Endorsements for
Living Beyond My Circumstances

Courage. Heroes. Crisis. Victory. God doing the impossible. A story-line for a novel? No. This is the life story of Deb Willows. She lets God shine through her circumstances. She honours her parents and friends as heroes...and especially honours God for giving her life and opportunity. Love and joy permeate her writing. In my own life I was deeply impacted by a mentor who had cerebral palsy. Deb is making the same impact in countless lives. This book will challenge you to walk in and live above your circumstances.

—Jerry E. White, PhD
(Major General, USAF, Ret; International President Emeritus)

Debbie Willows is on a journey that none would desire, but getting to know Debbie is a very encouraging experience. As a handicapped person, it is so challenging to see how, in her determination, no mountain is too high to climb. Her faith in the Lord Jesus is one to be espoused and causes one to realize that, with God, all things are possible. This book will be an encouragement to deny the negative and try those things made possible by God.

—Dr. Nell Maxwell

This story is about a young lady who can't walk or use her hands but who, by her strong character and unwavering faith in God, is living a life of positive influence and service to others. I believe this book will have a life-changing effect on all who read it. Debbie has never been a burden on anyone. She is truly an amazing inspiration to all who are blessed to know her.

—Dan, Deb's dad

I hope and pray that those who read this book will see the Deb we know: smart, loving, kind and generous, and one who has the ability to make friends. She puts God first in all she does. She once said to me, if she could walk, she would not be who she is. Deb is an amazing lady, and anyone who has the privilege of getting to know her will be blessed.

—Marg, Deb's mom

Growing up with Deb was like growing up with any other big sister. What my parents did, which was very unusual, was to tell Deb and us that she was normal and everyone else was disabled. We believed them and therefore treated her like any brothers would treat a sister. From my perspective, she was a fantastic sister. Deb laughed with us, cried for us and set an example of how to live.

—Terry, Deb's brother

I always thought of Deb as fun. (She would lick her Smarties and O'Henry bar so we wouldn't take them from her.) Deb was also really brave, especially as a teen attending a school of 2,500 students. As an adult, she is a patient leader. (We're quite impatient.) She has a pastor's heart, a real love for people—people I'd write off. She ministers to me and to my family. When we need advice or wisdom, we go to Deb. We all gravitate to her. She is an encourager, a servant of God. She has no other agenda but to serve the Lord and do His work.

—Danny, Deb's brother

I am pretty proud of Deb and what she has done with her life. Unfortunately, I work a lot, so I don't get to spend much time with her. But when she needs someone, I am there no matter what I'm doing. She is awesome, and I can't imagine having anyone else as my sister. Deb is the best.

—Sharon, Deb's sister

Table of Contents

Foreword

Deb Willows is one of those people you never forget—and those who know her well consider her a treasured asset in the Kingdom of Christ. That's because Deb knows something about what it means to be "more than a conqueror." She understands how to "welcome a trial as a friend" and "rejoice in suffering." She understands the virtues of perseverance and persistence. She lives out the encouragement Paul gave to Timothy to endure hardship as a good soldier. Such mandates from Scripture are tall orders for the average believer, and I'm convinced that is why God raises up special servants like Deb Willows. He understands the power of example.

And that's why Deb is such a treasure in the kingdom. She's the example we all need. Why? Well, those who endure greater conflict always have something powerful to say to those who face lesser conflict—and that's how I look at this remarkable servant of the Master. This woman is a rare jewel in the body of Christ, inspiring and encouraging all those who know her. And I trust you will come to know her well through this book, *Living Beyond My Circumstances*. The book you hold in your hand is filled with nuggets of biblical insight and wisdom, honed and shaped from years of living with a significant disability. So be encouraged. Be blessed. And see what *wonderful* things the Holy Spirit has to say to you through Deb's story!

Joni Eareckson Tada,
the Joni and Friends International Disability Center
(Summer 2012)

Acknowledgements

To my mom and dad, who loved me the way I was and never expected less of me. Thank you for showing Christ's love daily.

To Sharon, Dan and Terry, my siblings, who treated me like one of them. Thank you.

To Steph: Thank you for your friendship and help to accomplish another dream.

Celebrating the First Half Century

In 2011 I celebrated 50 years of life on earth, 50 years of joy, struggles and pain. Living with cerebral palsy was taking its toll on my body. My neck, shoulders and lower back are always in pain. Even so, each year was intertwined with God's faithfulness. I'd had 50 years to live for Him.

So, what do you do to celebrate half a century of life? You go big! We booked my dream vacation, a Hawaiian cruise, in September 2010 and planned the excursions we wanted to take.

"How do we get Deb on the tours?" asked Heather, friend, attendant and travel companion.

"Like always; we just do it." Pretty much my mom's answer to everything.

I'd taken many trips with only my parents to help, but they weren't as young as they used to be. Five of my friends volunteered to save up and come along. My poor dad was the only man in the group.

On March 26, Katie, Holly, Heather and I left Huntsville, Ontario, at 5:00 a.m. to drive to the Lester B. Pearson Airport in Toronto. Sylvia drove from London and met us there. We then flew to San Diego, where we connected with Mom and Dad. Esther was to fly in later.

Exhausted but unable to sleep, around 4:00 the next morning I asked, "Syl, is Esther here yet?"

"Not yet."

What's happened to her? Is she going to make it on time?

Not long after, there was rustling in the hall. "Syl, I think someone's at the door."

Whew! It was Esther. Her flight had been grounded in Atlanta, and she'd had to get another to San Diego. She was tired, but she made it.

The salt air tickled my nose as the eight of us boarded a cruise ship bound for Hawaii.

Over the next two weeks, each friend took turns helping with my care. It's one thing to assist in my home, but trying to help me shower or get to the toilet on a rocking ship...that's a whole new world. My wheelchair and I ran into many walls because of the rough seas. Without my power chair, I was totally reliant on my travel companions for everything.

When we arrived at the first island, we were greeted warmly by nationals who placed leis of shells around our necks while others danced to Hawaiian music. The tinkle of the shells and the rhythmic drumming filled my ears. It brought tears to my eyes. *I'm really here!*

We had 14 days of food and crazy fun. We toured four islands. We saw beautiful gardens and Waikiki Beach. My friends even helped me walk into the water. We attended a luau, saw the Grand Canyon of the Pacific and toured the Ocean Center in Maui. We enjoyed the many activities and abundant food aboard ship. We even had cake on my 50th and my dad's 73rd birthdays. Amazing!

Months after my birthday, on Friday, July 1, I was walking my dog on the road. (There are not sidewalks where I live.) It was busy, being the first long weekend of summer. A glistening black BMW swerved toward me. I thought, "I'll need to watch out for these crazy city drivers."

My brother Terry stuck his head out the window. A grin spread across my face. The family got out of the car to greet me, stopping traffic in both directions. They were in town from Vancouver.

That Sunday my family threw a surprise party for me. They put on a spread fit for a queen. Seventy people from all over came to celebrate. I was blown away. I caught up with friends—some I hadn't seen in years—including my grade eight teacher. I was in awe. God blessed me richly.

Dream 50th birthday in Hawaii, 2011

CHAPTER ONE

Go for the Gold

"See what my daughter won?"

The patrons looked up from their Big Macs and McNuggets to see what all the fuss was about. We were in New York, and earlier that day I'd set a world record swimming the 25-metre freestyle. My dad was grinning from ear to ear. And while my cheeks were burning, I was grinning too. Even the cashier got in on the fun.

"Would it be OK if I took the medal to the kitchen so the rest of the staff can see it?"

"Sure," I said.

When I'd graduated from high school, I prayed, "God, please don't let me lead a boring life." Was I in for an amazing adventure!

I participated in sports such as floor hockey in school but didn't know I was on the road to becoming a Paralympic gold medalist. On June 1, 1984, I could hardly sit still. My transportation was arranged. My bags were packed. And my swimming gear was stowed, everything including extra towels for me to sit on so I wouldn't slide out of my wheelchair when I was wet. Family and friends stopped by to wish me well.

The excitement was too much. Come 6:00 a.m., I was still wide awake, wondering what the next month would be like. In the morning I left for a week of training at the University of Windsor in preparation for the Games.

A couple of hours later, Doug, Canada's head coach, handed me a package. "Your uniform, Willows."

This is really happening.

Pretty much exhausted, I slept well that night. And it's a good thing too. The organizers had prepared a full schedule. Two hours of swimming before breakfast. An hour of slalom, an hour of field events and an hour or two of soccer before supper.

"I think you should take Friday off," Vicki, my coach, suggested.

I frowned at her and shook my head.

"Debbie..."

"Fine."

It was probably for the best. Having cerebral palsy (CP) meant I tired easily at the best of times. (Cerebral palsy is a neurological disorder caused by damage to the motor control centres of the developing brain either before or during birth. It neither worsens with time nor is contagious.)

On Saturday the athletes and their coaches boarded one bus while the other was filled with our equipment: two wheelchairs for each athlete, one everyday chair and another sports specific chair; spare parts; etc. We drove to Detroit so we could catch a plane to Newark. When we exited the airport, my heart began to pump faster. My eyes widened. The Paralympic Games bus was waiting for us.

After making our way through the congested New York streets, we arrived on Long Island. Immediately, the athletes went through an accreditation process. An official photographer took our pictures. After the day of travel, I looked like the dog's breakfast.

"Wear your ID at all times."

I sighed. Just one more thing to take in stride.

The thrill of practicing at the venues where the Games would take place was offset by the intimidation of being examined by a therapist and two doctors I'd never met before. This was part of the classification process. My muscles tensed and my mind raced, but I knew it was necessary. Each athlete's disability is different, and the Paralympic Committee wanted to ensure the playing field was as fair as possible. Talk about sensory overload.

"President Reagan is coming to the opening ceremonies. We're going to have to frisk those in wheelchairs and have those of you who can walk pass through a metal detector."

Are you kidding me?

Though I understood the importance of tight security, because I have spastic limbs that don't always do what I want them to it was very difficult to co-operate while being frisked. It was quite the process, but after approximately four hours, the 1,750 Paralympians and their coaches were cleared. The Games could begin.

"And now the team from Canada."

What a thrill to enter Olympic Stadium with my teammates, 14,000 spectators in the stands! It was a good thing I was sitting down or I might have collapsed.

"Are you Debbie Willows?" asked a member of the British men's team. He pointed toward the fence. "Your parents are over there."

I don't think he heard my thanks as Vicki propelled my wheelchair in their direction.

"Everything's all right," I said to the member of SWAT who stepped in front of me. (As I mentioned, there was security everywhere.)

"I didn't think you were coming until the 18th," I said to my mom and dad.

"They let me start my vacation early," Dad said. "It isn't every high school teacher who has a daughter in the Paralympic Games."

After hugging my parents, I rejoined my fellow athletes.

Over the following 12 days, records would be broken, some dreams fulfilled and others shattered. Undoubtedly, people's lives would be changed forever.

My heart began to race as the flags were raised and the torch was lit. Breathless, I realized I was representing my country. But even more importantly, as a Christian, I was also representing my God. What a show! What a day! What a dream come true!

The next day, I rolled up to the starting position, took the boccia ball, and tossed it toward the jack. Boccia is played by those with CP and other similar disabilities. Athletes throw a red or blue leather ball as close as possible to a white ball or "jack" on the court of a gym floor. My arms don't always co-operate; the ball doesn't always go where I want it to. That day, however, was a good day—a very good day. I sat as tall as I could and thrust my shoulders back as they placed the bronze medal around my neck.

The course was laid out the following day for the wheelchair slalom. The event is judged on accuracy and speed. This would be difficult at the best of times, but with strangers watching and heart pounding, I had to rein in my racing thoughts and focus on the course. I was the only competitor driving my chair by mouth, and although I didn't win a medal, I did come in fourth.

"I'd like to relax in the pool," I said to Vicki later that day.

"I think that's a good idea."

My body began to relax, but my mind was uncooperative. *What am I doing here? Who do I think I am? I can't handle it anymore.* Then I remembered the truth. I was a Paralympic athlete. I had been selected to represent my country on the international stage. I *could* finish what I'd started.

The new day brought a new outlook. The turmoil in my stomach was caused by excitement, not fear or uncertainty. Vicki held my feet, and I waited for the gun to go off. I felt so free in the water. No wheelchairs. No restrictions. No limitations. With all the strength and control I could muster, I pushed off and gave it my all. Twenty-five metres and one minute, seventeen seconds later, I set a new world record for the freestyle.

Yahoo!

Wait! What?

The pool was divided in two lengthwise. I needed my father's and Vicki's assistance to exit the water. What I expected was their help. What I didn't expect was to be thrown back into the water on the far side of the divider where there was more room to help me out. After the exhilaration of winning gold, it was a rude awakening, one I look back on with a smile.

On Saturday I participated in two field events. I won second in the precision throw and third in the distance throw, which is something like shot put. Another day and two more medals.

The next day I was waiting for the soccer game to begin. My coach had gone to get us some food, and I realized I needed to use the washroom. What could I do? There was no way I could manage on my own, and Vicki would not be back for a while.

My mom. She could take me. She'd done it thousands of times before, but this was different.

"I'm sorry," said the police officer, "but your mother doesn't have the proper clearance."

"Clearance? To take my daughter to the washroom. I'm her mother."

"Yes, ma'am, but rules are rules."

I was becoming very uncomfortable. "Isn't there something we can do?"

"Well," the officer said, "I could escort you."

I looked at my mom and she looked at me. She shrugged.

"If it's the only way..." I said.

That was the first and only time I've had a police escort to use the washroom.

Being a team sport, soccer presents unique challenges. Each wheelchair must meet specific standards so no athlete is at a disadvantage. Wheelchair soccer is a cross between murderball and hot-rodding. It's crazy, but fun...most of the time.

Crunch!

Those within earshot grimaced as the two chairs collided and Joe's foot broke. He refused to get it taken care of until he returned home. He didn't want to miss participating in the men's swimming events scheduled for later in the week. Such is the determination of a world-class athlete.

Before I'd left for New York, I'd received a new wheelchair.

"Make sure you don't smash the chair, Deb," my dad said.

He sure changed his tune. Above the noise of the athletes vying for the ball and the cheers of the fans, my father's voice rang out. "Go for it!" Concern for the chair was long forgotten!

Though we won against Great Britain, the U.S. team played aggressively and secured the gold medal. Canada won silver and Great Britain bronze.

Between events, I spent time with my parents. We went to Long Island Beach, did some shopping, went out for supper and hung out in their hotel room. The hotel manager even sent flowers when I won gold.

Before the closing ceremonies, my parents packed my power chair in their car and headed home. We hugged goodbye, and I watched them drive away.

As I watched the flame go out at the end of the ceremonies, I sunk further into my chair and sighed. I felt like a deflated balloon. What an emotional rollercoaster ride it had been. And yet, I knew one thing: I wanted to work like crazy in order to qualify for the Games in Seoul four years later.

After a little sightseeing, we made our way to the airport. We flew to Detroit, where we caught a bus for Windsor.

"Hey, Deb," my brother greeted me when I rolled off the bus. I could almost taste my mom's homemade cooking as we drove to London.

"It will be good to collapse into my own bed."

I should have known by his grin that something was up. It seemed my family had no intention of allowing me to quietly slip back into my pre-Paralympics routine. Friends and family swarmed around me when I arrived home.

"Congratulations, Deb..."

"To think I knew you when..."

"Our very own celebrity..."

That night I sank into bed with a grin on my face and a song in my heart. It was an amazing trip, an amazing dream. God gave me the ability each day to compete for Him.

If I ever had the opportunity to participate again, I decided, I would do some things differently. I had been so focused on the competition I hadn't taken time to make friends. I didn't give this much thought until I returned home. It isn't always easy to find the right balance.

In a very real sense, the medals I won are worthless. But when I share my faith with others, now that is pure gold. If back on that June day I did not swim my race, how many opportunities to share God's love would I have missed?

Receiving a silver medal, 1984

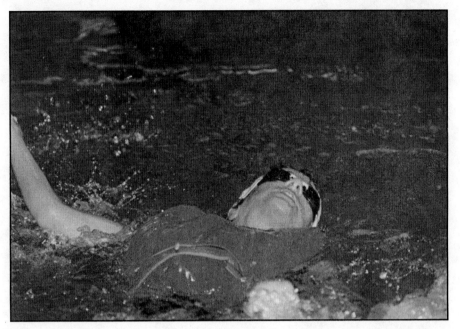

Swimming the backstroke

CHAPTER TWO

International Adventures

Nightmare in Belgium

"No, you don't understand. You *are* going to allow all of us on the plane and you *are* going to assist us." The coach was taking slow, controlled breaths in an attempt to keep his voice at a reasonable level.

We were returning home from Belgium, where I'd refereed at the 1993 World Boccia Competition. It was great to meet up with my brother Dan, who was there working at the Operation Mobilization office. He was able to join me in Antwerp and when I travelled to Brussels. When it was time for me to return home, he secured my wheelchair in a large crate to ensure it would reach Canada in one piece. Since I didn't think I'd need it, I left my local currency with him. Not the smartest move ever.

The weather was a problem in Brussels, and we'd been on and off planes several times in hopes that it would clear. It's hard enough for people without disabilities, but factor in our struggles with mobility and the fact that our wheelchairs were unavailable and you have the makings of a nightmare.

"Oh no!"

I looked out the window at the Brussels airport and saw the snow falling. They received an inch and a half, and by 6:00 all flights were cancelled.

"And what happens now?" the coach asked an airline official.

"Let me see what I can do."

He soon returned and informed us that they would put us up in a local hotel for the night.

"Good. Because we can't stay here."

"And to make it easier, you can take one of the wheelchairs from the airport."

The coach's mouth dropped open. "One? You're kidding me, right?"

"No, sir. That's all we feel we can spare." He spread his arms, lifted his hands palms up, and shrugged his shoulders. "Is there a problem?"

"Do you not realize these eight men and women," the coach gestured in our direction, "are unable to stand on their own?"

"Let me check again," the airport employee said.

"You do that."

The airline did allow us to borrow more chairs, but there weren't enough for all of us.

When we arrived at the hotel, the coach told us to wait where we were. He would go in and check on the accommodations. He was back in less than 10 minutes. He was shaking his head and mumbling all the way back to van.

"You are not going to believe this."

"Just tell us what's going on."

"They gave our rooms away and had no rooms available—none."

"Then what are we going to do? Spend the night at the airport?"

I shivered. I was tired. And I was cold.

"They gave me directions to another hotel."

"Let's hope they have room for us."

"Let's hope."

We pulled to a stop outside a hotel in an older section of the city. The good news was that they had vacancies.

"Thank goodness."

But before I could get too excited, I realized they had only one elevator—a very small elevator. So, to end the day's adventure, Jen, my personal assistant for that trip, had to prop me up against the wall, press the button for our floor, and charge up the stairs with the wheelchair so she could be there when the door opened.

"You really should get some sleep," Jen said when we were settled in our room.

"I know, but I really want to get in touch with Mom and Dad and let them know what happened. I don't want them going to the airport before they have to."

I spent a couple of hours trying to get through until I was just too tired to even punch in the numbers.

We had to be up early so we could be back at the airport in time.

"This is not happening," I said when I learned one of the boccia players had slept in and we would have to wait for her. I was more than ready to go home.

I thought back to our accommodations in Antwerp. Because there wasn't an airport in Antwerp, we had to fly into Brussels. The facility we stayed in was actually an institution for the disabled and had strict policies. We were not allowed to make or receive phone calls, and the doors were locked precisely at 8:00 p.m. There weren't even crash bars that would allow us to exit in case of emergency. My assistant had to crawl out the window—in her white pants, no less—in order to walk Lego, my service dog and constant companion. At least our experience in Belgium wasn't so bad in comparison.

I felt Jen's hand on my shoulder and heard her calling me back to the present. "Deb, Deb...you in there?" she asked.

"I was just thinking back over the trip."

"Ready to get home?"

I nodded.

Thankfully, we got to the airport in time. In fact, we were escorted past other passengers and taken by elevator directly to our gate. That was when we were informed they would only take one disabled person per flight. The coach would have none of it.

When we arrived in Paris, they gave us a calling card so we could contact our families. I finally got through to Mom—at 4:00 in the morning. It was 10:00 a.m. local time.

"Mom, I'm sorry to wake you."

"Is everything all right?"

"It is now, but we're still in Paris."

"What happened?" I could hear the concern in her voice.

"It's a long story. I'll tell you all about it when I get home. I just wanted to let you know. Love you."

"Love you too."

Jen hung up the phone for me. "Tammy," I said to a fellow boccia player, "you don't have to call home."

She shrugged. "Why?"

"Your dad and brother are sleeping at my parents' house." I laughed.

"Seems they didn't know what to do when we didn't show up at the London airport, so they went to my house."

Tammy and her mom looked at each other and laughed.

Paris really is a beautiful city, and we had five hours to kill. It would have helped if I'd kept some of my money. Thank goodness the airline picked up our restaurant tab. Although we didn't get to see the city, customs did stamp our passport. I can at least say I've been there. By 3:00 that afternoon we were on our way home.

"Woohoo! We're home."

No one was happier than Lego. When you travel with a service dog, you need to get airport security to take you outside so the dog can go to the bathroom—once on the airplane, he must hold it. Therefore, he's given very little to eat or drink. If he could've talked, I'm sure he would have asked me if we ever had to travel by plane again.

And the crate with my chair? Well, I was without the wheelchair—and the clothes Dan had packed with it—for the next week. The airline mistakenly sent the crate to Boston before forwarding it to London.

Runaway Wheelchair

Four months after I refereed at the National Games held in Vancouver, BC, in 1993, I had the privilege of travelling with Jen to Sheffield, England. I enjoyed refereeing there, but that wasn't the most exciting part of the trip.

We had a day off during the competition, so Jen and I decided to take the train to Birmingham. I had been so impressed with the wheelchairs used by the British team that I wanted to touch base with the people who manufactured them. While we were there, I picked up some spare parts.

"That was a good day," Jen said when we arrived back at the Sheffield train station.

I agreed.

We got situated on the platform, and Jen placed the box of spare parts on my lap. Everything would have been fine, except the train whistle blew and I jumped. The box of parts went flying.

"Here, let me pick those up," Jen said. She got to work but forgot one important thing: to secure the brakes on my wheelchair.

I was screaming for help in my mind, but nothing came from my lips as I began to roll toward the moving train. I crashed into the side of the train with such force it bent my footrests. Angels must have been surrounding me that day. Even though my seatbelt wasn't fastened, I stayed in the chair.

"Deb, I'm so sorry. How can I ever make it up to you? I can't believe that happened."

I was speechless during our ride back to the hotel. I'm sure I was in shock, but I was also contemplating just how good and gracious God had been.

SURGERY AND A WEDDING

When I got home in February, I went to the doctor's for a routine test.

"Deb, I have something to tell you." The doctor pulled up a chair in front of me. "I suspect you have endometriosis, and I want to send you to a specialist next month."

Endometriosis...really?

When I got the name and address of the specialist and the date I was to see her, I made all the necessary arrangements. After the examination, I went home to await the results. Because it's difficult for me to get to the doctor's, they usually give me the news over the phone. I was alone when the specialist's office called.

"Miss Willows?"

"Yes, that's me."

"We're calling to confirm that you do have endometriosis and will need surgery."

My head was spinning when I got off the phone. When the shock wore off, the tears came. However, in less than an hour, I came to the realization that God hadn't let me down in the past and He wasn't about to start. He would see me through.

My parents came home from holidays on the Saturday, and by Sunday we had tracked down my surgeon's home number. She graciously accepted the call, and we discussed what would happen next.

"We'll do exploratory surgery to see the extent of the endometriosis," the doctor said, "and then a follow-up procedure will likely be scheduled." She paused briefly. "Debbie, you'll probably need a hysterectomy."

My parents and I talked at length with her, and she agreed that it would be best to perform the hysterectomy at the first surgery. It didn't make sense to subject me to two procedures.

When I was 16, I had been scheduled for a hysterectomy. At that point, nothing was wrong—except that I had CP. Routine sterilization was common for people with disabilities. I didn't want to go through with it, because I hoped to, one day, have children. When the whole controversy hit the news, the hospital dropped me from the surgical schedule for fear of the backlash. At 35, with a diagnosis of endometriosis, things were different.

On April 1 I underwent the procedure. I was in the hospital for nine days and was abundantly thankful for family and friends who could meet my needs. The nursing staff did their best, but they weren't trained to assist patients with disabilities. I was especially touched by my brother Terry.

"Hey, Sis," he said before the surgery, "if you need a transfusion, I'm your guy. I don't want you getting some stranger's blood. You never know what can happen with this whole contamination thing."

Although I missed celebrating Easter with my church family, I didn't miss my brother Dan's wedding. The last week of May, I flew to Belgium with my friend and assistant Cathy. Terry, his wife and their six-week-old baby came with us. Mom and Dad had flown over the month before to help with the preparations.

"What a great camp," Cathy said.

"Yeah, Grace arranged for us to stay here," I said. "This is where they'll hold one of the ceremonies."

"One of them?"

"They have to have a civil ceremony at city hall. Then they'll come back here for the Christian service."

"Really?"

"Uh-huh."

The ceremony at city hall was performed in French, and the city employees who attended were dressed in traditional clothes from the 1800s. After the half-hour ceremony, we did pictures, ate lunch, then headed back for the second ceremony, which Grace's father, Jonathan McRostie, officiated.

My brother Terry, who was a pastor in Belleville, gave the message at Dan and Grace's wedding.

Two days later, Cathy and I, Terry and his family, and my parents flew home. Dan and Grace joined us the following Saturday. We held a second reception for them at our church in London.

"Isn't her dress beautiful?" one of the ladies said.

"Lovely."

It was a great evening, but Grace and I woke up the next morning very sick. It seems a week and a half of wedding celebrations proved to be a little too much.

Carrying the torch in London, ON, 1996

CHAPTER THREE

A Slight Setback

Before my days as a Paralympic athlete and boccia referee, we faced some challenging times. My parents have often shared with me their first memories of our little family.

"Why can't we hold our little girl? Is she all right? Everyone else gets to hold their babies."

My dad stood beside her, holding Mom's hand and doing his best to comfort her as they watched me through the window. "She's in intensive care. They're doing all they can for her."

Because of oxygen deprivation at birth, I spent the first seven days of my life in the neonatal intensive care unit at Victoria Hospital in London, Ontario. Although they could visit me, neither of my parents could hold me. At the end of the week, the nurse placed me in my mother's arms for the first time. Mom smiled down at me, then hugged me close. For the next four days, the nurses brought me to my mom daily.

"Mrs. Willows."

"Yes."

"We're releasing you and the baby tomorrow."

Her smile lit up the room.

My dad came to get us the next day. "We're going home, Debbie." His eyes sparkled.

Like all new parents, they showed me off to family and friends. Everything seemed to be fine. It wasn't until I was six months old that they realized something was wrong.

"Aren't babies supposed to be sitting on their own by this time?" my dad asked.

Mom nodded.

This was just the beginning. They took me to doctors all over the city, seeking answers. Finally a diagnosis was made.

"Your daughter has CP," the doctor said. After a brief pause, he added, "You should put her in an institution where they are equipped to care for children with her condition. It would just be too hard for you." Another pause. "Then you can get on with your lives."

My mom's eyes filled with tears.

"Absolutely not," my father said.

In the days following, my mom and dad had many serious conversations.

"Why do you think God gave us a daughter with a disability?" Mom asked.

"I really don't know."

My mom hung her head. "How can we cope? And how will we explain it to everyone?"

Dad shrugged. "We've been Christians for a long time. We go to church and try to do what's right…"

After a lot of discussion and soul-searching, my dad came to a conclusion. "This is the child God gave us, and we have to accept her as she is." And that was the end of it.

My parents got down to the task of raising me the way they would any child—with, of course, some special considerations.

When I was four I was fitted with metal leg braces to help me walk. I used them every day until I was 13. *No fancy shoes. Just ugly brown boots. And a two-hour car ride to Hamilton whenever I outgrew the braces and needed new ones.*

"Mom, they're cold." I shivered.

"I know, Deb, but you've got to wear them—even in the winter."

"Dad, they're so hot."

"Debbie…"

I sighed. There was no use arguing. My parents did their best to understand the challenges I faced, but they did not allow me to get away with feeling sorry for myself.

As I got older, I developed problems with my hips. The doctors could perform a procedure, but they said there was only a 20 percent chance of success. If they didn't do the surgery, I would have to spend my waking hours in a wheelchair for the rest of my life. Since I would end up there anyway—and since I really didn't like the braces—I chose the wheelchair. It was the right decision. It gave me much more freedom, and getting ready didn't take nearly the same amount of time.

Walking wasn't the only thing that gave me trouble.

"Hold still."

"I'm trying. Really I am."

We discovered the only way I could get a decent haircut was for me to lay my head on the kitchen table while a friend of my mom's cut my hair. My dad built a special chair for me to sit in that helped. And in time, with lots of therapy and the right medication, I gained control of my head and neck. I can now type, write and paint by mouth.

Most people don't like going to the dentist, and I can identify. Though there was a specially trained dentist on staff at the Thames Valley Children's Treatment Centre, Mom had to come with me and keep me still. (Since moving to Huntsville, I've had to go to a regular dentist. It takes a lot of effort to keep my head from moving—especially when he's coming at me with the drill. There are times when I leave the office exhausted and in tears.)

At the centre I underwent just about every kind of therapy imaginable. Physical therapy to develop gross motor skills, speech therapy to help me make myself understood and occupational therapy to teach me to dress and undress myself and to accomplish other everyday tasks.

"Debbie, you won't be allowed to go home until you fasten this row of buttons. I know you can do it. Keep trying."

I tried...and tried...and tried again. I just couldn't do it. My arms moved when and where they wanted—and they didn't want to fasten buttons.

Eating with my hands was also out of the question, never mind using a fork and knife. The occupational therapists tried to teach me, but my body just couldn't get the message. One evening at dinner, I hit my plate. It flew past my dad and landed in the living room, getting food every-where. Despite objections, I began to eat my way: bringing my mouth to the plate.

"Would you look at that?"

I noticed the stares and pointed fingers when we ate out. I didn't want strangers to criticize my mom for allowing me to eat this way. However, I was thankful she did. It gave me a measure of independence.

"Ma'am, what would your daughter like to eat?" the waiter asked.

"You can ask her. She's right here."

If I wasn't being noticed—and criticized—I was often treated as completely invisible.

But like my mom, my kindergarten teacher, Mrs. Miller, helped me learn to do things on my own. She gave me a mouth-stick that was specially designed for me. I could use it to hit the keys on a typewriter. I could write! She also encouraged me to read to the class from her copy of the Dick and Jane reader. I've always loved books and learned to read when I was four or five. My heart soared to discover the things I could do.

Like any child, I didn't want to be left out. When I was seven, I developed a condition I found more debilitating than CP. I began to get migraines. When one came on, I couldn't eat. Worse than that, I had to stay in bed. I missed many events.

"Mom, I want to ride in the Model T." Despite the fact that my eyes were squeezed shut, a tear slid down my cheek.

"Let's just get you into bed so you can rest and get rid of that headache," my mom said as she ruffled my hair.

Even when I didn't have a migraine, I would watch my siblings play in the yard with their friends. I often wished I could join them, but I learned to enjoy being on my own, reading, knitting and painting.

I was later surprised to learn my sister actually envied me. While she had to bundle up and play outside in the snow, I didn't. She didn't understand, but when I was out in the cold, my muscles tensed up. It made it virtually impossible to move. I would just have to sit there in the snowbank. There was no way my wheelchair would make it through the snow. It was like trying to manoeuvre through sand. Impossible.

One day my sister decided to run away.

"Where's Sharon?" I asked.

"She's outside playing." My mom continued preparing a batch of homemade cookies.

"I don't see her."

Mom glanced out the window. She looked from left to right and back again.

"It's snowing pretty hard," I said.

Mom nodded. After she scanned the yard a second time, she dropped the ball of dough onto the baking sheet, wiped her hands and called down the stairs. "Dan, come up and watch Debbie and the boys. I'm going out to look for Sharon."

"What?" he asked as he climbed the basement stairs, but she was gone.

Half an hour later my mom and sister came through the front door, shivering and covered in snow.

"Don't ever do that again," I heard my mom say.

"I ran away 'cuz I thought Deb was your favourite. She always gets to stay inside when it snows," Sharon said before she headed to her room.

When I was eight, I began to attend a special orthopedic class at Oxford Park Public, a "regular" school. Mrs. Smith was very nice, but she didn't want her students to move on. I was in that same grade 2 class for five years. It had nothing to do with my level of intelligence. We were simply too busy to accomplish much academically. On Tuesday morning, we would go to the treatment centre. On Wednesday, it was swimming. We did arts and crafts on Thursday. And on Friday morning, we had music class.

Swimming was the best. I was free in the water and loved it, but swimming for your country is nerve-racking. After all, how could someone who couldn't even dress herself propel herself through the water? I had to wear a flotation device because my muscles were always tight. I could not float; I sank like a rock. I always had to swim on my back because I couldn't turn my head to take a breath. In competition, my coach was allowed to hold my legs in the start position until the gun went off. She couldn't touch me again until the race was over. My legs were strong and I could push off. It took years to make my arms move the right way.

My arms couldn't do much when I started, but the more I practiced and used arm weights, the more my arms could do. Because I persevered, I was able to participate in swimming events on the world stage. I was also able to do several other things over the years I never would have been able to do if swimming wasn't part of my therapy as a child, things such as operating my power chair with my hand. Now I swim only for fun when it's warm. I can no longer do the backstroke because it hurts my back too much. When I was young, I only knew I wanted to be more like my sister and brothers.

"Dad, school is fun, but I want homework. Sharon, Terry and Dan get homework, and I'm older than they are. I want to go to real school."

"We'll see."

Gerry Brock, a family friend and a teacher, also believed I could do more. After many tests, he and other professionals came to the conclusion that I could work at a grade 7 or 8 level.

"Now we have to find you a school," my mom said.

With the help of the school placement committee, which included representatives from the Children's Treatment Centre and Sandy Posno, a lady who would become a very important part of my life, my parents and I began the search for a school that would be willing to take me. But where? Disabled students were segregated at the time. My parents may have taught me to see CP as a slight setback, but was there anyone else who would agree? Who would take a girl with CP and integrate her into a class of able-bodied students? Not only did the school have to be wheelchair accessible, the principal had to agree.

In September of 1976 I began at Byron Southwood Public School. The principal, Doug Dickson, took a chance.

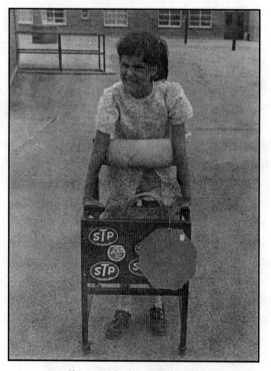

Walker made by Debbie's dad

CHAPTER FOUR

Real School

My dad and I were at Byron Southwood getting things ready for my first day of real school. Dad was building a ramp and adding a grab bar to the girls' washroom. The whole time I was thinking, *I wonder why we're doing this if I'm going to be healed tonight.*

That evening we went to a healing service at the London Gardens, a hockey stadium often used for public meetings. It was packed. The sick. The disabled. The curious. We were all there hoping to witness—or experience—a miracle as the "faith healer" spoke and prayed. While I believe God can and does perform miracles, I did not receive a healing touch. I had lived with CP since day one, so it wasn't really that hard on me. It's all I've ever known.

The truly hard thing was Sharon's response. She'd been hoping so desperately for an able-bodied playmate—and for the taunting about her "retarded" sister to stop. She was devastated when we arrived home and I didn't jump out of the car. She burst into tears, ran into the house and went flying up the stairs to her room. Mom went in and talked to her, and I waited for Dad to help me out of the car. My heart broke for her.

September came, and it was time for me to start school.

"But Mom-mm, I want to go to school tomorrow."

"I know you do, Debbie, but the teacher wants to tell the other students about you before you get there."

I rolled my eyes. "Oh, all right."

I was used to being treated differently, but I just couldn't understand why the other kids stayed away from me for the first couple of weeks. Finally, one brave soul solved the mystery for me.

"So," she asked, "how long do you have to live?"

I stared at her for a moment. "What did you say?"

"The teacher said you have some condition and won't live as long as the rest of us."

I had to laugh at this misunderstanding, as I did at many others. It was either that or allow myself to become frustrated and angry. I found out later the teachers and staff thought I had muscular dystrophy. Muscular dystrophy, unlike CP, does worsen over time. It, too, refers to a group of conditions. Muscular dystrophy involves muscle weakness and the loss of muscle tissue.

Even when we got that cleared up, there was still a great deal of misunderstanding.

"Mrs. Willows, I was wondering," one of the teachers asked my mom, "is it safe to touch your daughter?" Apparently he thought CP was contagious. In the end, I taught them as much as they taught me.

Despite the initial confusion, I made many good friends. They were helpful and understanding and never made me feel like I was a burden. Their friendship didn't solve all my difficulties though. Because the other students went home for lunch and I couldn't, I had to eat alone. There were certain classes I couldn't attend because they were inaccessible to someone in a wheelchair. Physical education was downstairs: no elevator. Home economics and music were in portables: no ramps. At times I was lonely, but I didn't feel particularly left out—most times.

"Honey, try to sit still while I help you get ready."

"But I'm too excited to sit still. Today's the field trip."

"I know..."

"Did you remember to sign the permission form?"

"You handed it in with your money. Remember?" Mom said as she brushed my hair.

"I know. I just can't believe it. I'm actually going on a field trip."

I was grinning all the way to school.

"I'm sorry, Debbie, but you can't go with us today," Mr. Cook said.

My mouth dropped open. "Why not?" I asked.

"It's just not going to work with your wheelchair and the bus and all."

Then why did you take my permission slip and my money?

I didn't want to protest too much. After all, they were making many special concessions for me. That knowledge didn't help much as I tried to hold back the tears as the last bus pulled away. I spent most of the day in the school library.

A few months later, our class went on a trip to the Grand Theatre. This time I was not left behind. The rest of the class went on a bus, but the principal drove me and a friend in his car. What a delight to be included!

Although missing a field trip was just one of several disappointments, I still loved school. I could hardly wait for each new day. I was learning so much. Mom had to practically tie me down to make me stay home when I was sick. There was one day, however, when I almost wished I was sick.

"How can Mrs. Posno do this to me?"

"Now, Debbie," my dad said, "you wanted to be just like everyone else."

"But people don't always understand me when I'm speaking directly to them. How are they ever going to figure out what I'm saying from the front of the class?"

"You won't be up there alone," my mom said. "Cathy's working with you."

"Cathy can't do all the talking. Mrs. Posno said I had to try."

"Just do your best," Dad said.

When the time came for a classmate to wheel me to the front of the class, my head was spinning and my stomach was doing back flips. *Maybe I'm not going to graduate from grade 8 after all.*

"Why TV is bad for you..." Cathy began.

She completed her portion of the debate, and then it was my turn. I took a deep breath and started to read my well-researched, carefully timed speech. When I looked up, I noticed my classmates weren't laughing or whispering. They were actually paying attention.

"Deb, that was great," Mrs. Posno said. "You spoke very clearly. Good job!"

Over the years, I've spoken at Youth for Christ events, church functions, service clubs and sports banquets. I owe it in part to a teacher who saw the student, not the wheelchair.

I had more fun in two years at Byron Southwood Public School than I'd had in the previous five. There was a goofy grin on my face during the best parts of graduation day. We were dismissed at noon to get ready. Mom took me to get my hair done, and when the time came, she helped me get into the pretty pink dress she'd bought for me. I felt like a princess. Could it get any better?

"Why does she have to go to Saunders? It's such a big high school—over 2,000 students. She won't have the help she needs," my mom said to my dad.

"Don't worry, Mom. I'll be fine."

I was about to embark on the next phase of my journey. I learned more about independence and socialization in high school than ever before. Mrs. Boon, the librarian, became a great friend.

"I'm not sure I can do this," I said when she asked me to stamp and sort the vertical files.

"I'm not sure either, but let's give it a whirl." Dad made this a lot easier by forming a handle for the stamp that I could hold in my mouth without damaging my teeth.

My many new friends also helped in countless ways. They wheeled me from class to class and assisted me at lunch. They used carbon paper to make a second set of notes. If that didn't work, they took the time to hand-copy them for me.

My friends couldn't help but laugh the day my teacher stood too close to me. At times I unexpectedly flail my arms. This particular day, I whacked Mr. Cook right in the stomach. I pressed my lips together to keep from joining in the laughter.

This teacher wasn't the only casualty along the way. When I was in grade 9, I received a special wheelchair I could drive with my chin. I practiced controlling it by trying not to hit people as I bombed around Westmount Mall. I hadn't mastered the controls the day we had a fire drill. On my way out of the classroom, I ran over my science teacher's foot. Oops!

I not only had difficulty controlling exactly where I went, sometimes I forgot I could go on my own.

"Deb, what are you doing?" my friend asked.

I laughed. "Oh, yeah...I guess I don't have to wait for someone to push me to my next class, do I?"

I joined Campus Life when I was in grade 9. Campus Life is a ministry of Youth for Christ. It's a program designed to help teenagers live life to its fullest in all areas: relationally, physically, emotionally, intellectually and spiritually. They accomplish this through events such as Bible studies, trips and events and student leadership.

When I was in grade 9, the organization planned a Christmas wrap-up in Toronto. Students from all over Ontario would come to learn from the guest speakers, praise and worship along with the worship team, and simply have a great time together.

"Please, Mrs. Willows. Let Deb come with me. I promise to take good care of her," my friend Leslie said.

Mom shook her head. "Well, I don't know."

I made my eyes as big as possible. I may even have cocked my head a little. I assured my mom I'd be fine. Eventually she relented—reluctantly. She never would have agreed if she knew what was going to happen.

"Oh, come on. We can make it."

I sat at the top of the escalator looking down.

"I'm not sure about this."

"How else are you gonna get to the meetings?"

"Well, I guess..."

With two of my male friends in front of the chair and two behind, we headed off downstairs.

The music. The speaker. The hotel. The shopping. Doing normal teenage things. I enjoyed it all. Well, maybe everything except the escalator. To this day, I don't relish the thought of ever riding one again.

It was even better for my mom. She learned there were things I could do that not even she dreamt were possible. In fact, much of my life has been about seeing "the impossible" come to pass.

"Congratulations, Miss Willows."

Who would have thought that a little girl who the doctors didn't think would amount to much of anything would successfully complete five grade 9 courses—with honours?

OK, let's go for six next year.

While I was enjoying academic and social success, there were still several hurdles to overcome. Public buildings back then, including schools, were not wheelchair accessible. Thankfully, my dad was a shop teacher at Saunders. If my wheelchair broke down, I could call him. If my bus didn't show up—which was often the case—he was there to take me home. If I needed money for lunch..."Dad?!"

It's a good thing he was available, especially for the first little while. The school didn't provide staff to help with my personal needs like going to the washroom. My dad, being the handyman he was, put up railings in the girls' washroom. He also did other things around the school to make life easier for me. He saw to it that my locker was across from the wood-working shop so he could help me when needed. He made a special wooden shelf for the back of my chair to carry my supplies. Members of the football team were assigned to carry outside those of us who could not make it on our own in case of a fire drill. My dad was in charge. No chance of any funny business.

Dad wasn't always available to help me, nor was it always appropriate. One day I got some exciting news.

"Mom...Mom...guess what?" I said as I entered the house after school.

"Calm down, Deb," she said and looked up from the dishes. "What is it?"

"They've hired an assistant." I could hardly get the words out.

Mom wiped her hands on the tea towel and walked over to me. She placed her hand on mine. "Who's hiring an assistant?"

I was bouncing up and down. "The school...the school hired an assistant to help me and the other disabled students...not just every now and then...all the time."

"Oh, Debbie!" She hugged me.

Jan, the assistant, didn't have an accounting background. It was so much fun trying to explain to her how to draw the symbols as I dictated my answers. I'm sure no one else had such a good time writing exams.

Accounting was fun for other reasons too. That's where I met Jenna. She was one of the students who took notes for me and helped me at my locker. She and I enjoyed spending time together and would go to one another's homes. Jenna was quiet and shy and didn't have many other friends. We changed all that at Campus Life. She especially loved the concerts. Her life was changed because of Campus Life, as were the lives of many others. It was awesome to see God work in their lives. And He was certainly at work in mine.

"I want to take seven courses next year."

"Grade 11 is going to be harder," my mom said.

"Absolutely," Dad agreed.

"I know I can do it."

My mom looked over at Dad and then back at me. "We know you can too."

Grade 11 was, indeed, more challenging, but the Shriners made it more manageable. My art teacher was a member of this organization, which helps children with a wide variety of needs. (They are often most well-known for their children's hospitals.) The school approached them about raising money to help buy a computer that would make it easier for me to do my homework. They did more than help. They arranged for a camera crew from the *London Free Press* to follow me around for a day. My friends thought I was some kind of a celebrity. The Shriners purchased a Commodore PET, one of the first personal computers, for me. In both grade 11 and 12, I took computer programming and had to learn computer languages. Jim, the computer teacher, had been very involved in getting the computer for me. He also went out of his way to help me learn to use it.

"Jim," I said, "you really don't have to come over after school to help me."

"Sure I do, Deb. And I will come Saturday morning before my daughter's dance class."

"Really?"

"Absolutely."

I networked with the University of Western Ontario's computer. Talk about painfully slow, but it was better than keying the computer cards for programming. Even so, it was extremely helpful and enabled me to do well for the remainder of my days in high school. Grade 11 brought other changes as well.

Physical education class had never been an option for me. That year the school introduced a special program for students with disabilities. It was a great opportunity to show the teacher what we were capable of. We learned to play floor hockey and baseball. We exercised and danced. Time in the weight room was my favourite. We even used the trampoline.

"Are you sure you want to do this?" one of my classmates asked.

"Of course."

I lay on the trampoline, and they began to jump. It was amazing—until I landed awkwardly and twisted my knee. It swelled up like a balloon.

I love to joke around about almost everything, and this was no exception.

"Mrs. Brown, I need the period off."

"And why is that?"

I nodded toward my knee. "I got hurt in gym—on the trampoline."

Her expression was priceless.

Sports weren't my only interest as a teenage girl. Rob, a friend from church, gave me a flower at Valentine's, something I didn't expect from any boy. We enjoyed each other's company and spent time together with our friends. The week before graduation, he asked me to meet him after math class.

"Deb," he asked, "would you like to go to the graduation dinner and dance with me?"

My jaw dropped. "Wow! Really?"

"Really."

Every girl dreams of having a date for grad. I didn't get much sleep for the rest of the week. And that made things rough. Not only was I attending the dinner and dance, but I was participating in the Regional Games for the physically disabled, my first competition. There would be athletes from communities from Windsor to London, Ontario. There was no need to qualify to participate. I'd signed up for five events, and they began the day after grad. I got home at 1:00 in the morning and had to be at the Robarts School for the Deaf by 8:00 a.m.

"Really? I won?" I asked after completing the wheelchair slalom. I came in second in my two field events. My parents picked me up at 11:00 p.m. I almost fell asleep on the 30-minute ride home.

"Are you ready to go?" I asked my mom the next morning. "We have to be at Robarts at 8:00 a.m. We can't be late."

Although I didn't qualify to go on to the next level of competition, participating in the games was a thrill. I promised myself I would do better next time—and I did.

Vicki became my coach the following year. We trained hard, and it showed. I qualified for the Ontario Games, where I won two gold medals for swimming and wheelchair slalom and two silvers and a bronze for the distance and precision throws.

I enjoyed going to sporting events as well as participating in them.

While Rob and I attended the occasional movie and church event together, I remember one hockey game in particular.

"Ready to go?" Rob asked when he came to the door.

"I am."

I looked over my shoulder and told my parents I would see them later.

"Have a good time," Dad said.

When we got to the arena, my friends and I thought it would be more fun if I could sit in the stands with them. A few of the guys carried me to my seat and tucked my wheelchair out of the way. After the game we waited until many of the other spectators had left before my friends went to get my chair.

The stands continued to empty, and still no one came back to get me.

"Where could they be?"

Jenna shrugged her shoulders. "I dunno."

"Uh, Deb?" Rob said as he bounded up the steps.

"Yes?"

He wouldn't look me in the eye.

"What is it, Rob?"

"We...um...well...the thing is...we can't find your wheelchair."

My eyes got wide.

"What are we going to do?"

"Don't panic. It's got to be here somewhere."

"It better be," I said. "I don't want to have to explain this to my folks."

"Me neither," Rob said. "We'll keep looking."

They split up and searched the arena. It was almost empty before one of them found my chair. Apparently someone had used it to prop open a door.

"Whew! That was a close one," I said.

From time to time, the people at church saw Rob and me together, and sadly, some of them misunderstood our relationship—and the Scriptures.

"Now, Debbie," an elderly woman said, "you know what the Bible says about being unequally yoked."

I didn't correct her, but that reference has nothing to do with those who are able-bodied and those who are not. Besides, Rob and I were only friends. We had no intentions of marrying. He felt God wanted him to be a missionary to Africa, and I didn't want to do anything to stand in his way.

I continued to excel in school and graduated from high school with honours. I earned both an accounting diploma and a business certificate. Some parents who taught at the school presented their sons and daughters with their diplomas. My dad was going to, but he got too busy giving a speech, telling the audience about what it had taken to get me to that day. He also spent a great deal of time thanking those who made it possible. I don't think there were many dry eyes in the place.

The principal ended up handing me my diploma. I wanted to prove the doctors wrong. I wanted people to see God's strength in me. Although I couldn't shake the principal's hand or wave at those clapping for me in the audience for fear of hitting someone, my heart was light. I wanted to show them CP was truly only a slight setback, and with God's help, I did.

Debbie's world opens with first computer

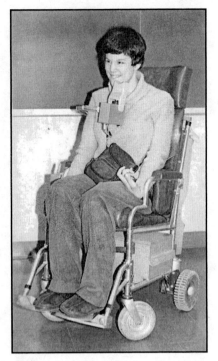

Debbie's first power wheelchair brings freedom

CHAPTER FIVE

Family Life

"This weekend we're all going on a hike to earn our next badge."

I loved being part of Pioneer Girls. I'd earned every badge and even done the work for extra credit. All the girls worked hard, and it was great to be part of the group. But I had no idea how I was going to earn the hiking badge. There was no way I could make it over the rough ground with my braces, and going in my wheelchair wasn't an option.

"What are we going to do?" I asked my mom on our way home.

Mom didn't answer but kept looking out the windshield.

"Mom..."

"Hm...what?" She looked over her shoulder at me.

"How am I going to earn my hiking badge?"

"Don't worry about it, Deb. We'll figure something out."

"Mom!"

"Debbie, don't whine."

"Yes, Mom." I was only seven, but I knew when a conversation was over.

My dad and I were sitting in the dining room at supper.

"Dad, tell me again about when you were a little boy."

"You want to hear that story again?"

I smiled and waited.

"We should start when your grandma was a girl and first came to Canada from England."

"Not long after the Titanic sank, right?"

"That's right. She was adopted by a nice family."

"Then she grew up and married Grandpa."

"She did."

"And when you were three, Grandpa died."

Dad laughed and shook his head. "Who's telling this story?"

"I...uh..."

Dad grinned.

I waited a minute or so, but when Dad didn't say anything, I continued. "Grandma never got married again."

"No, she didn't, Deb. She raised me and your Uncle Jack all by herself. We took any job a boy could get to help pay the bills. She had boarders stay in the house to help cover expenses. She did not have much to live on and raise two boys."

I thought for a minute and then said, "I remember the one lady who lived with Grandma. She was grumpy!"

"Yes, she was." Dad laughed again.

"Grandma was a strong lady."

"Sort of like you." Dad winked.

"Ah, Dad..."

"Later I got the job as a pattern maker, and that helped with the bills. Then, when your mom and I got married, we lived with Grandma for a year."

"Was that hard?"

"It sure was," Mom said when she came into the room.

The rest of the week went well, and I didn't think much about the hike—not until Saturday morning, at least.

"Mom," I said from my place at the table.

"Uh-huh," she said without looking away from the stove.

"Today's the Pioneer Girls' hike."

"Yes it is."

Mom turned off the element and left to call Sharon and Danny for breakfast. Terry was already strapped into the highchair across from me.

"What the..."

The next thing I knew I was lying on my back. I turned my head in time to see my dad leaving through the kitchen doorway.

"Daaaaad!"

"Dan, put your daughter's chair the right way up," my mom said as she came back with my brother and sister in tow.

"Ah, do I have to? If I don't, there'll be more breakfast for me."

"Dan..."

"All right. All right."

It was no fun feeling helpless, but my dad loved to tease, and he treated me the same as he did everyone else.

After breakfast, Mom put me in the car.

"Why don't I have to wear my braces today?"

"Oh, you'll see." That's all she said, and we were off.

When we pulled into the parking lot, the girls, their moms and the leaders were all arriving and gathering at the entrance to the trail. I still had no idea how I was going to fulfill the requirements for the badge.

Mom came around the car and opened the door. "We're here."

"Uh-huh."

Mom put me on her back and said, "Here we go. You didn't think I was going to let a little thing like a hiking trail keep you from earning your badge, did you?"

We had a great day, and I'm glad I didn't weigh any more than I did. Not only did we complete the hike, but I actually got to start a fire using the stick I usually used for typing. My dad rigged it so I could use it to strike a match.

He was always making me things: a holder to keep toast upright so I could eat it; an ice cream cone holder (that was pretty great); puzzles with extra-large pieces...if it could be made from wood, my dad could make it.

Both Mom and Dad showed me time and again just how much they loved me. When they look back on it, they don't think they did anything particularly noteworthy, but I know differently.

"Do you want to go to the corner store, Sharon?"

My sister looked up from the Barbies she was playing with. "Think Mom'll let us go after I got in trouble for trying to sneak the pop up to our room last night?" She stuck out her lip. "It was your idea. I don't know why I always get in trouble."

"I'm sorry, but I'm sure Mom will let us go."

"Go where?" Mom asked when she entered the living room.

"Can Sharon and I go to the corner store? Please."

"Well, I don't know."

Sharon gathered up her toys. "I'll put everything away before we go. I'll be careful. I promise."

Mom went to her purse and took out her wallet. "Could you get me some milk while you're there?"

Sharon took off down the hall to grab a jacket. "Thank you. Thank you. Thank you."

Mom smiled and put the money in the bag attached to my wheelchair. "You two be careful."

I smiled. "We will."

Sharon and I always had a good time going to the store together. She was only eight, but she'd already learned how to manoeuvre my wheelchair like a pro. Everything went fine until we were almost home.

"Just tip it back a little farther," I said. "The wheels are still getting caught on the curb." (Curb cuts hadn't been invented yet.)

Sharon followed my instructions perfectly, but the angle was just a little too much for her. My weight and the weight of the wheelchair made it impossible for my little sister to hold it any longer. The wheelchair tipped on its side—spilling me into the street. My sister tried hard to get the wheelchair upright and put me back in the seat, but it was just too much for her. It was especially scary when I noticed the city bus headed right for me.

Thankfully, our neighbour saw what had happened and came flying out of the house. I was soon right-way up and on my way home.

It was a while before Mom let us go to the store alone again.

Trips to the corner store weren't the only ones we took. We had a cottage in Haliburton and enjoyed vacationing there as a family. Some nights we'd sleep in tents, the girls in one, the guys in the other.

My brothers shared Dad's love of practical jokes.

"Shhh, do you hear that?" Sharon asked.

"I don't hear anything," I said.

"I think Danny and Terry are trying to sneak up on us."

I strained to hear. "Yeah, you're right. And I think Dad is with them."

Next thing we knew, there were frogs in the tent, and the tent was collapsing. Of course our friends and Sharon scrambled out, but I was stuck.

When I turned my head, I was staring into the eyes of the biggest bullfrog I'd ever seen. I screamed. I'm really not sure who was more frightened, me or the frog.

This was just one of the many times my brothers got the best of me. To this day, Terry grins as he remembers some of their antics.

"Mom and Dad never told us Deb was disabled," he explains.

My dad bought a Winnebago motorhome so we could travel around Canada and the United States. We had a great time and saw many things. Like most families who have the opportunity to go, we enjoyed exploring Disney World in Florida, especially the second time.

"Can you believe this?" My dad was grinning from ear to ear.

Mom patted his arm and smiled. "It's better than it was last time."

"Much better! Deb, do you want to go on the Pirates of the Caribbean ride?"

"Sure, that'd be great."

There was no doubt Dad was even more excited than I was that they now allowed people in wheelchairs on more of the rides. As the ride continued, Dad became more and more excited. It was fun to watch.

"Did you enjoy that, Deb?" he asked as we exited the ride.

"I did. Thank you."

Dad began pushing me faster and faster.

"Dad...Daaaad..." The exit ramp was fast approaching. However, it wasn't flush with the walkway—and my seatbelt wasn't fastened.

It was too late. The front wheels of my chair caught on the ramp, and I flew out of the seat and landed on the ramp. Thankfully, nothing was broken.

Poor Dad! He felt as bad I did—maybe worse.

Even with our little mishap, our trip to Disney World was a lot of fun and it was good to see that those in wheelchairs had access to more and more attractions.

Joni Eareckson Tada has been in a wheelchair since 1967, when she suffered a spinal cord injury as the result of a diving accident. She, too, has seen the change in accessibility. She was—and still is—my inspiration. One of the highlights of my childhood was seeing her in Kitchener.

Sun sparkled on the dew-kissed grass as the robins announced the arrival of a new spring day. My parents, my siblings and I all piled into the motorhome and headed for Kitchener. Only Mom and I had tickets for the auditorium where Joni would be speaking. The rest of the family was planning to spend the day at the park.

I was 16. Having read Joni's book, I was very interested in meeting a famous person who was in a wheelchair—like me.

Joni talked about the pain and joys of being disabled and how God can use even people with disabilities for His glory. Like a thirsty sponge, I soaked up each word. Joni explained how God uses pain to make us more like Him and how our real home is in heaven. Her story was a huge encouragement to me.

She greeted each of us as we left the auditorium. When we finally got to the door, Joni asked me my name. I was speechless—for the first time in my life. I had so many questions I never got to ask.

Our family went out to eat before driving home, but I couldn't enjoy it. I'd developed a migraine from all the excitement. I was too sick to eat. Mom and I were in the washroom when I started to cry.

"All I want is to be able to go places and not get sick. Isn't it enough that I have CP and can't walk or use my hands? Why do I have to get these headaches? I just want to have fun with my family and friends."

Then Mom said something I'll never forget. "Deb, you have to be happy with what God has given you—even if it's pain and sickness. He only gives us what we can handle. Remember? That's what Joni was talking about today."

Mom understood what she was talking about. Her mom left when she was only 7. When she was 16, she had to leave school and get a job to help support the family because her dad became ill. Mom got married when she was only 19, and 18 months later, I arrived. My mother understood what it meant to live a difficult life.

My mom loves me greatly, but that doesn't mean it was easy having a daughter with CP. She had to toilet me, bathe me, dress and feed me—while caring for three younger children. She had to do her best to ignore those who criticized her for making me do things on my own. I'm so grateful she did. Because of it, I became increasingly independent.

Meeting
Joni Eareckson Tada, 1986

Many years have gone by since that trip to Kitchener. I still get migraines that make me sick, but I know God is in control and He is with me through every moment of pain and joy. I also know He gave me a very special mother, who showed me how to rely on Him.

CHAPTER SIX

A Daughter's Love

Just how deep is a daughter's love? In June 2005 we discovered the answer to that question.

My dad had kidney problems most of his life. When he was in his mid-20s, he contracted a bad case of strep throat that put him in the hospital. He became so sick it damaged his kidneys. In September of 2004, it became clear they'd begun to seriously deteriorate. He had to travel from Huntsville to Orillia every few weeks to see a specialist.

"Deb, we need you to get a questionnaire together," Mom said when she and Dad got home from one of the appointments.

"For what, Mom?"

"If we can find a donor, the doctor has agreed to do a transplant."

I prepared a form for family and friends to complete if they were willing to be considered as potential donors. Although I wanted to be tested, because of the CP and the lengthy recovery time that would be needed I was not eligible. My sister Sharon, however, was a different story.

"You haven't done as I've asked," the doctor said at a subsequent visit. "Therefore, we are going to start dialysis next week."

"Wait just a minute," my mom said. "We *have* done what you asked. Plus, you said if we could find a donor, my husband could have a transplant."

"Yes, I did," he said with a little less arrogance.

"Good. We will have a donor by next week."

And it turned out to be more than wishful thinking. On their way home, my parents got a call from Sharon. The doctors had found out from her blood work that she was a good candidate. They wanted her at Toronto General the next day for further testing.

"Can you take me?" she asked.

"Of course."

Talk about timing! The doctors in Toronto discovered she would be a perfect candidate. After that, Sharon had to have a physical and see a social worker to make sure she could handle the procedure, not only physically but emotionally as well.

Things had to move quickly. The longer they kept Dad off dialysis, the better his chances of responding well to the new kidney. However, his condition was deteriorating, and the doctors didn't know if they could wait. The date for surgery was set for Monday, June 6. By God's grace, Dad avoided dialysis.

"No, Mom, I want to be there."

I was visiting friends in London but insisted on meeting them in Toronto. I didn't think it was a good idea for Mom to face this on her own.

I caught up with Mom and Sharon at the hospital after Dad was settled in his room and started on anti-rejection medication. After visiting hours, Sharon, Mom, and I headed to the hotel to try to get some sleep. Knowing what lay ahead, that was almost impossible. It was particularly difficult for Sharon. Because of the extent of the surgery, it is actually more difficult for the donor than the recipient. She would be in a lot of pain. Knowing that ahead of time made it all the more challenging. Plus, she had to be at the hospital by 6:00 the next morning.

I decided not to go to the hospital until 8:00 a.m. That would give Mom and Dad some time alone together. Dad was taken to the operating room at noon. Sharon had already undergone the two-hour surgery to remove her kidney. When she was taken to her room, I stayed with her while my mom sat in the waiting room.

"Hey, Sharon," I said when she started to come around.

"Uh..."

"Did you know Prince Andrew was touring the hospital?"

She gave a half grin. "Oh yeah? You can invite him up, and I can show him my stitches."

I burst out laughing. Apparently my sister was still pretty heavily drugged.

The surgeon entered the room where my mom was waiting for news about Dad.

"Mrs. Willows?"

"That's me." My mom stood up as the surgeon entered the waiting room.

"Everything went well. Your husband is in recovery. Someone will let you know when you can see him."

My mom smiled. "That's great." Under her breath, she muttered it was hard to see her daughter in so much pain.

Sharon is a strong woman. It didn't take long before she was up and doing more than she should have been.

My dad did remarkably well. It all began at 6:00 a.m., and by 4:30 in the afternoon he was back in his room.

"Mom, they're both OK. Let's go for a walk," I said.

Mom nodded. "That sounds like a good idea."

"Look, a Red Lobster." We enjoyed our first real meal of the day, then headed back to the hospital.

We spent our time going back and forth between Sharon's room on the fourth floor and Dad's on the seventh. I was with Sharon when a nurse brought Mom in around 8:00 p.m. She was just too tired to find the right room.

"Time to head back to the hotel," I said.

Shortly after we got to our room, the phone began to ring. Even though we wanted nothing more than to collapse into bed, it was encouraging to know people were praying. The calls didn't end until 10:30 p.m., and when we were finally able to get into bed, I was too tired to even pray. But I was convinced God would take care of everything.

"Guess who's here with me?" my dad asked the next day when Mom called from the hotel.

"Who?"

"Sharon."

"What? Did the nurses bring her up?" Mom asked.

"Nope. She walked."

"You're kidding," Mom said.

"You know our daughter."

Once we got back to the hospital, Mom visited with my dad while I stayed with my sister, and vice versa. Unlike my sister, Dad would have to use a walker, but he didn't allow that to affect his mood. It was amazing to see the difference in him. He was so rundown before surgery, but less than 24 hours after the transplant, he was bright and cheerful. He was even joking around with the nurses.

"Dad's back," I said with a big smile on my face. I had gone to find Mom in Sharon's room.

My mom agreed.

"And remember how they said he would be in ICU for a week?"

They both nodded.

"Well, they're moving him to his room—today."

Mom's eyes got round. She jumped up and bolted from the room.

Sharon was to be in the hospital four or five days. Even so, she wanted to go home in two, though she was in more pain than she'd anticipated. On Tuesday she enjoyed a couple of nice surprises. A friend of hers brought her children to see her. Plus, Dad had a friend deliver a dozen roses to Sharon's room as a thank you.

Our family members were not the only ones who thought she was special. On

Wednesday the lady in the bed next to Sharon's was discharged. After taking his wife downstairs, the lady's husband stuck his head back into the room.

"My wife told me what you did for your dad. I just had to come back and tell you that I think—we both think—you're a hero. Not everyone would do what you did."

The doctor discharged Sharon on Thursday. Sylvia, my good friend and assistant, and I were going to take my sister home. I wouldn't have been able to stay in Toronto when my parents needed me or get Sharon home if it wasn't for funding to pay my staff. It was just another one of God's rich blessings. I am independent by nature, but there are many things I couldn't do without my assistants.

And I am not the only independent one in my family. When Sylvia and I arrived on the fourth floor to help Sharon with her bags, she was coming down the hall, carrying far too heavy a load.

"Sharon," I said, "what do you think you're doing?"

We got her settled in the van and headed north.

We stopped in Barrie to eat and then saw to it that my sister was settled in her home in Huntsville. By the time I got to my place, I was so exhausted that I fell asleep sitting up with my glasses on. It took two full weeks for me to recover—and I wasn't the one who'd had surgery.

"Mom, how's everything going?" I asked during one of our nightly calls.

She had never stayed in Toronto by herself, and she was nervous. Mom was particularly wary walking the streets amidst crowds of people she didn't know. She always made sure to head back to the hotel before dark. It was a good thing there was a Winners store en route. Mom found it relaxing to pop in and do a little shopping.

"I'm not so sure about this," my dad said one night on the phone. "Here I am lying in a hospital bed, and your mom's out shopping. Does that sound right to you?"

We both laughed.

I arranged for some of my mom's friends to visit while she was in Toronto. That plus her shopping trips made her time in the city easier to handle.

Dad healed better than we could have hoped for.

"Deb, it's wonderful!" Mom exclaimed. "The doctors say your dad is doing so well they are discharging him on Saturday. He can stay at the hotel."

"You're kidding. Less than a week after surgery?"

"Uh-huh."

For two weeks, Dad had to check in at the hospital every Monday, Wednesday and Friday. At the end of the third week, my brother Dan picked them up. Dad was home for Father's Day weekend. What a blessing! Throughout this time, I continued to receive emails from people all over the world asking us how Dad and Sharon were doing and assuring us of their prayers. All the support was such a moving experience.

"The doctor says I can drive myself." Dad could be at home on weekends, but he had to spend the weekdays in Toronto.

By the middle of August, he was only travelling to the city once a week. Soon it was every other week, then once a month. Dad now goes every six months and will continue to do so for the rest of his life. He has to travel to Orillia monthly for blood work. Any medication he needs has to be authorized by the transplant team. It has been seven years since his surgery, and my dad is still going strong. He has had other complications, but not because of the kidney. It's simply because, like the rest of us, he's getting older and lives in this crazy world.

Sharon recovered well, although she did do things sooner than was advisable. For example, she was on the roof shingling—the week after surgery. Not only that, she tried to move a closet storage unit by herself the day she got home. She can be a little nutty sometimes.

It was difficult on her children. She was a single mom, and Kristal, Danielle and David weren't able to stay together when Sharon was in hospital. They were glad to have her home and did their best to keep an eye on her. Children are such a blessing.

Two months after dad's transplant, Dan's fourth child, Malcolm, was born. Because Grace, his wife, was due to deliver that summer, I had been concerned that both the transplant and the baby's arrival might happen at the same time. Instead of staying with Mom, I would have been watching several nieces and nephews. As always, God's timing is perfect. We were all around to enjoy the new family member.

Family reunion, 2012

CHAPTER SEVEN

Minds of Our Own

"I want to do that!" I squealed.

Even as a young child, I dreamt big. I watched Olympic swimmers on television and knew I wanted to do what they did. I always enjoyed swimming. It was good therapy, but more than that, the water was the one place I was free. Free from the pull of gravity, as long as I wore my lifejacket. Free from my wheelchair. Free to be truly independent.

When I learned there were Paralympic Games for athletes with disabilities, I knew my dreams could become reality—if I worked hard and refused to give up. But that's how I was created. God gave me the determination, the inner strength and the ability to go for the gold.

Just like everything else I've been able to accomplish, it meant hours of hard work and a great deal of support. I'm so thankful for family, friends, teachers and others who stood behind me. They didn't try to curb my enthusiasm—even when they had no idea how I could reach my goals.

I began competing in 1981 in my hometown of London, Ontario. I did not qualify for the Provincials that year, but in 1982 I qualified at the Regionals and went on to my first Provincial Games. At the 1983 Provincials, I qualified for the 1984 Paralympic Games.

"Good for you."

"Congratulations!"

"That's fantastic!"

"I knew you could do it."

During my first trip to Belgium, in 1986, I had the privilege of representing Canada at the International Games for the Disabled. Travelling is always an adventure for people with disabilities. This trip served to reinforce that.

My eyes bugged out when we got to the airport in Brussels. "We're supposed to fit in *that*?"

The van that was waiting for us was much too small to transport the athletes, the coaches and the wheelchairs—two for each competitor, since we used power chairs for the Games and manual chairs after the others were packed away for the return trip.

We left the wheelchairs behind and headed for Gits, Belgium. We were in for another surprise when we reached the institution where we were being housed.

"These wheelchairs must be the first ever built," I said.

They had canvas seats, support for only the lower back, and no footrests. It was a long and painful 12 hours while we waited for our equipment to arrive.

We also brought spare parts. Inevitably, our chairs would get damaged because the baggage handlers were not trained how to treat them properly. (They still aren't.)

"Really? We don't have the part we need to fix my chair?"

"Nope, sorry."

It was a good thing the people of Belgium liked Canadians. It was amazing what you could get in exchange for a Canadian pin.

"Which cot would you like?"

Oh, this is going to be interesting.

They had set up six to eight cots in each classroom. Not exactly the most luxurious of accommodations. Our hosts showed us the one shower inside and directed us to several others outdoors. However, there was no hot water. Cold showers are no fun at the best of times. For someone with CP, it's even more unreasonable. My muscles would immediately tense and become virtually useless.

"You'll never guess what we found," one of my coaches said.

"What?" I asked.

"A shower..."

"And?"

"It's in the therapy room—and it has hot water."

"Really?"

"Yep."

When we could, we'd sneak away and use it.

Despite everything, the people of Gits did a good job hosting the

Games. The opening ceremonies were fun and, as always, solidified the reality that I was competing on the world stage.

My first event was the wheelchair slalom.

"Unbelievable!" I felt as if I was going to take wing.

After two runs, I'd set a new world record. I also set records in the 25- and 50-metre freestyle. It was the first time organizers included the 50 metre, so I had the privilege of setting the standard.

"You've done well, Deb. Three world records. That's amazing!" my coach Doug said.

"I know but fifth in boccia. That's disappointing."

Over the years, the Lord has taught me a lot about competing. While it's always thrilling to earn a medal or set a record, it's more important to find satisfaction in doing my best. For me, that often meant competing with a migraine. God gave me the strength and determination to work through it. Events take place when scheduled—headache or no headache. One time I competed with a dislocated elbow. Now that was painful, but God got me through. He can use it all for His glory: winning, losing, migraines, dislocated joints, whatever.

I wanted to glorify God when I competed—and when I socialized between events.

"Willows, you coming?"

For many of my fellow athletes, relaxing meant going to the local pub and drinking large quantities of beer. I'd learned that it was important to spend this time with my teammates.

"Coke, right?"

I nodded. I appreciated the fact that the others knew I didn't drink alcohol. Even more so, I appreciated the fact that they didn't tease me about it.

"Hey, Deb, can I talk to you for a minute?" one of them asked.

"Of course."

We separated ourselves from the group.

"Why are you so happy? Does it have something to do with your faith?"

"Let me tell you about my best friend, Jesus."

I never forced what I believed on anyone, but if they wanted to know, I was ready to share. God can use both our words and our actions to make an impression on others.

One day a group of us certainly made an impression.

"We can do this," Kim, one of the coaches, said. She had rented a car so we could take a trip to Bruges.

I looked the car over. I turned my head one way and then the other. "You really think we can all fit in there?"

"You're Olympic athletes. You can do anything."

Maybe not anything, but all of us did squeeze in—seven adults and four wheelchairs. They did have to be disassembled for the trip, but we did it.

What a great diversion from the pressure of the Games! It was so much fun.

"Debbie, you had visitors," one of the athletes told me when I returned.

"Really? Who?"

"A Mr. and Mrs. Posno came by to take you out to dinner."

"I'm sorry I missed them."

But it was good to get away for a few hours.

I'd often see the staff of the institution whispering amongst themselves. I'm sure they didn't know what to make of us. They were used to working with disabled people who did as they were told. Not that we weren't thankful for their help, but we were so glad for the merciful soul who went to a local restaurant and brought back spaghetti, the best meal swimmers can have the night before race day. It really was a welcome relief from the ham and cheese we were served morning, noon and night.

"Mom, I have a favour to ask," I said one night when we were talking on the phone.

"What is it, Deb?"

"Could you have spaghetti for me when I get home?" Hers was the best.

"Um...OK!"

Just hearing her voice made me homesick. Only Teresa came with me. Although I love hearing new languages and learning about new cultures, there's something to be said for the familiar sights, sounds—and tastes—of home.

I enjoyed being in Belgium in 1986. It was good to reconnect with people I'd met in 1984 at the Paralympic Games. And I knew I was going to work hard over the course of the following 24 months in order to qualify for the 1988 Paralympics in Seoul.

Extra training pays off with two gold medals in Gits, Belgium

CHAPTER EIGHT

A World of Extremes

The Windsor Indoor Games were always held at the end of March and were open to all athletes. They were "the first official unofficial games" of the season.

In 1987, I earned two gold medals in swimming and silver in boccia. It was a good start to the season. More importantly, I did well at the Regionals in June. I earned three golds in swimming and a bronze in boccia. Qualifying for the Paralympic Games looked better and better.

I did well in boccia and precision boccia at the Provincials in North York. I'd also qualified for the wheelchair slalom but had no way to get my power chair to the Games.

One day I wore a T-shirt that a member of the British team had given me at a previous meet. Prince Andrew and Fergie were special guests at the Games. They noticed the T-shirt and stopped to talk to me.

"It was very nice to meet you," Fergie said before they moved on.

"You too." I'm sure I was glowing.

It would have been nice to have Prince Andrew present me with a medal for the slalom, but you can't change what you can't change, and our brief visit was almost as good.

The organizers of the Provincials held a banquet on Saturday night after the meet. I enjoyed the food and the conversation. But that wasn't all.

"And now, we would like to name this year's Athlete of the Year," Doug said. The conversation ceased, and the athletes, coaches, and other attendees turned toward the microphone.

"Ms. Debbie Willows, could you please come forward?"

It had been a big year for me, and it wasn't over yet.

The Can-American Games were held on Long Island at the same location as the 1984 Paralympic Games.

"It's good to be back."

"And this time you're the team captain."

I took a deep breath. It was an honour, but it was often difficult to decide who played and who didn't. Although we came in fifth for team boccia, I did well personally. I set a new world record for the 25-metre freestyle and came in first in the 50 metre.

When I got home I said to my mom, "I'm going to need a new coach before I go to Windsor."

"How about posting an ad at the Y?"

"That could work."

Laurie responded to the ad, and we set up a meeting.

"I'd be happy to travel with you and help you train."

"And I'm thrilled that you're a believer."

Laurie came to church with me and got along well with my family. These are always pluses in a coach.

"Deb, I've got news," Laurie said one day. She pulled a chair up in front of me.

"What is it?" I asked.

"I'm not going to be able to be your coach after the triathlon."

"Really? How come?"

"My husband got accepted to teachers' college."

"That's great." My disappointment for myself gave way to excitement for them.

"It is, but the college is in Thunder Bay."

"A little far to travel, huh?"

"Just a little."

I'd miss her, but I knew God would provide.

Esther was a boarder at my parents' home while she studied pre-health science at Fanshawe College.

"Deb," she said one evening at supper, "I'd like to volunteer to be your coach."

A smile spread across my face. "Thank you."

Most of my training was trial and error. There hadn't been much research on how to prepare disabled athletes for sporting events. Most of my life I've been a pioneer, trying new things and breaking new ground. This was no different.

The time came for my trip to Korea for the Paralympics.

Esther didn't come with me. She felt it was too much time to take away from her studies. Thankfully, Laurie was available. We flew from Toronto to Los Angeles with team members from Ontario. The next day all the Canadian athletes and their coaches made the 15-hour flight to Seoul.

"Have we landed on a different planet?" I asked Laurie.

"You'd think so."

The police had to hold back the cheering crowd. They treated us like the world-class athletes we were. It took my breath away.

"Wow! Look at that," Laurie said as we made our way through Paralympic Village. It had everything we needed. Places to shop. A cafeteria. A chapel. And more.

The Games were well organized. We spent a week going through the classification process, training and adjusting to the time difference. Day was night, and night was day. These were the first Paralympic Games in which they implemented drug testing. It was an encouraging sign. It was just one more way they were treating us like "real" athletes. The Korean people were very hospitable and held banquets in our honour. However, there were disappointments along the way as well.

"I'm so sorry, Deb," Laurie said. "I know how much you wanted to participate in the swimming events."

"What can you do?"

It was the first year officials decided they weren't going to include events that allowed participants to wear lifejackets.

Despite my best efforts, I didn't win a medal in boccia or team boccia. The competition was very stiff.

"Did you see the chairs they were using in the slalom?" a team member asked.

"Who could miss them?" another said.

"I'd like to give one a try," I said.

"For sure."

The British team's new wheelchairs were smaller, faster and more maneuverable, giving them a definite advantage.

In the process of realizing I wasn't going to win any medals or set any records, I made some important discoveries. I was still Debbie Willows. God could still use me to do many things. I still had value. And I was still in His care.

It's a good thing I was learning these lessons. It gave me the courage I needed to call home, something I'd been putting off until I had good news.

"So, have you won any medals yet?" my brother Terry asked when he answered the phone.

"Not this time," I said.

There was a brief pause. "Then why are you calling?"

Only a brother...

Truth be told, I was glad my siblings didn't treat me differently because of the CP.

I had more lessons to learn before leaving Korea. We had some time to explore, and we came across people who lived on the streets with nothing more than a cardboard box for shelter.

"Laurie, look over there." I gestured out the car window.

"Oh, Deb," she said.

"We are so blessed." There were disabled Koreans begging on the streets. One man with no legs was getting around by pushing himself on a skateboard. I said a silent prayer for him.

On the brighter side, I enjoyed meeting people from around the world and trying new food—though I eventually got tired of rice and wondered if I could use it to affix tiles to the wall. It was fun visiting the markets and watching shoppers barter for merchandise. We even did a little bartering ourselves. Memories of Seoul will stay with me always.

Enjoying the moment in Seoul, Korea, 1988

CHAPTER NINE

Tally Ho!

Jolly good!

I'd always wanted to go to England, and in 1989 I would get the opportunity.

The trip home from Korea was something else. Instead of staying over in Los Angeles, we immediately boarded a plane bound for Toronto. I would never recommend flying 20 hours straight.

I could not, however, sleep for a month, the way every fibre of my body was screaming at me to do. While I had gotten as much bookwork done as I could before I left, there was still plenty waiting for me. And since people want to be paid for some odd reason, I had no choice but to get busy and do payroll.

"The sun's shining. It's a beautiful day. Why do you look like you're going to fall asleep at your computer?" Esther asked.

"Maybe because my body still thinks it's the middle of the night."

"How come?"

"I'm still on Korea time."

"Just one of those things if you're going to be a world traveller, I guess."

"I guess."

Somehow I got my work done.

"You sure you're up for this?" Esther asked.

"How often do I say no to a challenge?" I grinned.

"You have a point."

Only three weeks after returning to Canada, I participated in a triathlon in Ottawa. The triathlon included boccia, precision boccia and precision throw. I didn't win, but I did come in first in the individual boccia and second in precision boccia. I also had the opportunity to reconnect with friends who used to attend my church. That was nice.

God has given me many special friends and supporters over the years. The people at Union Gas were especially good to me. They raised money for my trip to Seoul. After I returned, they invited me to make a presentation about my time there. I was glad to do so.

"That was wonderful, Debbie. And now we have some good news for you."

I looked up at the Union Gas representative.

"Debbie, we'd like to do another fundraiser. We would like to buy you that new power chair."

"Oh, thank you!" I wore that grin for a long time.

As it turned out, Doug, one of my coaches, was able to bring the chair back from England when he returned from his business trip and vacation.

"It's beautiful," I said when the wheelchair was uncrated. "Only one problem..."

"The hand controls," my dad said.

"Yep."

"We can fix that."

"Really?"

"Sure."

So, once again, it was my dad to the rescue. He and an electrician friend created a control I could operate with my mouth. Now I owned one of the chairs the British team used to win the slalom in Seoul. It became more than a chair for competition. I used it every day. It was such a blessing.

I got to take my British-made chair when I went to the Robin Hood Games in Nottingham. My dad's mom was British, and I hoped to track down some of my relatives.

I was too busy participating in the Games to go searching, but God worked things out in an unexpected way. I had my picture taken with Robin Hood, and it appeared in the newspaper. A local woman saw it, noticed my last name, and came to the World Games Village looking for me.

"I'm so sorry, but I don't have time to visit. You could stay and watch my boccia game with my parents"—and she did. "My parents are staying at the dormitory. You could talk to them."

Through the course of the conversation, they learned she was a distant cousin. I went to England hoping to connect with family, and God saw to it that I did.

That was only one of many memorable things that happened while I was there. I did come in first in my swimming events, although I didn't set any new records. It's more difficult to swim in warm water.

Thanks to my new power chair, I took silver in the slalom. And the chair itself attracted a lot of attention. Representatives from the company that manufactured the power chair were at the Games. They were interested in the modifications my dad had made. When my events were over, we travelled to Birmingham with them to tour the company.

"Mom, Dad, look over there!"

"What is it, Deb?" my mom asked.

"Look at the workers."

"Yes?" Dad said.

"Some of them are disabled...and you know how hard it is for disabled people to find work."

This was a company I could do business with. While we were there, we worked out the details for me to become the sole distributor of their wheelchairs in North America. I was about to embark on my very own business venture. They agreed to send three chairs home with us.

On the way back to Nottingham, we took a side trip to Coventry. The rolling green hills. The thatched-roof houses. The sheep and goats. It was great to see the place where my grandmother grew up.

"It's just the way I imagined it would be," I said. I looked around the pub. Heavy English accents and the smell of fish and chips hung in the air. What a wonderful way to finish off my trip to England!

In August 1989, I participated in the National Games in British Columbia. I set new Canadian and world records in the 50-metre freestyle that, to my knowledge, remain unbroken.

I was in for more big excitement in the spring of the following year. I headed to Windsor with Keli-Lyn, a fellow athlete, and her family early Friday morning. My friend Ann had all my swimming gear and was supposed to join me after work. She was to be my hands and feet at the Games, but as a teacher's assistant, she couldn't get away earlier.

"Willows, there's a phone call for you."

I cocked my head. "From whom?"

"A woman named Ann."

I gasped.

"Deb, I'm so sorry," she said. She sounded like she might cry.

"Where are you?"

"I'm stuck in London."

"What?" I'm independent, but without a helper, I can't feed or dress myself—or go to the washroom.

"We had a huge snowstorm. I just can't make it."

I hung up. There was nothing to be done. But, as always, God provided for my needs. Laurie, my former coach, was helping with the classification process at the meet. She agreed to help me scrounge up what I needed.

"I have a towel you can use," one of my fellow athletes said.

"I've got an extra bathing suit," said another.

"And I have two lifejackets. You're free to use one."

Plans may change, but when I'm in the water waiting for the gun to go off, I have to clear my mind and focus on the upcoming few seconds. I was able to do so and I won all my swimming events.

Even so, I let out a huge sigh when I rolled through my front door at home.

In July, Ann and I travelled to Assen, Holland. They put us up in a modified army barracks. Though I'd stayed with seven others in the trans-formed classrooms in Belgium, I'd never shared accommodations with so many other athletes and their attendants.

There were no swimming events, but I did participate in boccia and took third in slalom. I also enjoyed our trips into town: shopping, tours, evening entertainment.

"*Dag*, Debbie. That means hello in Dutch. I'm Myjam, and this is my husband, Kees. We're helping at the Games this week."

These two volunteers took me under their wings. After they returned home, they sent me letters. What fun to receive mail while I was in Assen! After I returned to Canada, my dad was surprised that they called to make sure I'd arrived home safely. To this day, we keep in touch.

Nineteen ninety was the last year I participated in the Games as an athlete. I competed in the Regionals, the Provincials and the Nationals. Thanks to God, I finished strong.

Left: Power wheelchair results in bronze medal in Assen, Netherlands

Below: Throwing boccia jack ball

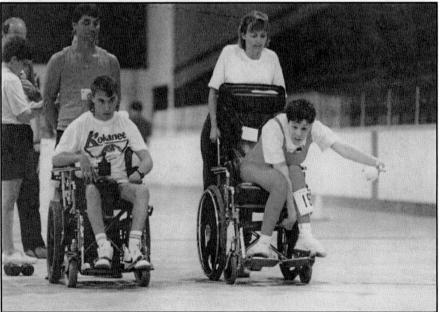

*On the podium in Assen, Netherlands, 1990, with friends
and competitors from England*

*Stopped by a Bobby for speeding on way to receive
a silver medal, England, 1989*

CHAPTER TEN

Beyond Competing

"Willows, you're a good athlete. But ref? I don't think so. You'll run over the ball." Other boccia refs would shake their heads. Who'd ever heard of such a thing: a boccia referee with CP and in a wheelchair?

"And why not?" I said to my mom. "I don't see any reason I can't become a ref. After all, who knows the game better than the athletes?"

"What's gotten you so riled up?" Dad asked when he entered the living room.

"She's been talking about becoming a boccia ref," my mom said.

"And why not?" Dad said.

I grinned. I knew my life would have been much different without supportive parents. So, off I flew with my sister to Portugal to take the three-day course, a course I later taught in Canada.

"Hey, Willows, I see you made it."

"Yes, I did." I was grinning from ear to ear when I arrived in Barcelona to ref in my first Paralympics. It was a challenge. The referees' accommodations were not equipped for the disabled. I had to ride with the athletes because the refs' transportation was not wheelchair accessible.

There were also other considerations. I had to get a smaller paddle to hold up to indicate which colour would throw next. Other people helped me measure the boccia throws for scoring. I announced the score verbally because I could not hold up my fingers. Since holding a pen in mouth required me to use my own pen, my helpers kept my pen handy for signing the score sheet. They also held the coin needed for the coin toss at the beginning of each game because I could not put things in or take them out of my pocket.

None of these hurdles seemed significant when I had the honour of refereeing the gold-medal game. Wow! Another first. I loved it.

As a group of Canadian athletes walked by, one asked me, "Wanna go to the beach?"

"How exactly?" I asked.

"They've constructed a wooden walkway just outside Paralympic Village."

"Cool! Let's go."

One evening I rolled into the dining hall only to find there were almost no available seats. There was a gentleman in clerical attire sitting in a wheelchair at a table by himself. I rolled over and asked if I could join him.

"Certainly."

"I'm Debbie Willows. I'm one of the boccia refs at the Games."

"Nice to meet you. I'm Jonathan McRostie. As you can tell," he gestured to his clothes, "I'm a pastor. I have the privilege of serving in the chapel at the Games."

Over our meal, we shared about our lives outside of sports. What a kind and gracious man!

"See you around," we said to one another before we headed in different directions. We did not, however, meet up again at the Games.

In 1993 my brother Dan went to Belgium.

"Hey, Deb, guess what?" Dan said one night when we were talking on the phone. "I'm working with someone who knows you."

"OK...I've been to Belgium, but I can't think of anyone who'd be with Operation Mobilization."

"I've been working as a personal assistant for a Jonathan McRostie. Sound familiar?"

"You mean the pastor I met in Barcelona?"

"The very same. We were talking and he began to tell me about the Canadian he met in Spain. I figured out he was talking about you. Crazy, huh?"

"It really is."

When I refereed in Antwerp that year, I saw Dan with Grace. I just knew when I saw them together they'd get married. And in 1996 they did. Funny thing...Grace was Jonathan's daughter. Amazing!

Jonathan was the European director of Operation Mobilization. Because he went to be with the Lord in 2011, the year before I completed writing this book, I wanted to include a further tribute to this godly man.

Born of missionary parents and educated at Moody Bible Institute and Wheaton College, both Christian postsecondary institutes, Jonathan followed his parents' footsteps into fulltime ministry. His original commitment to work with George Verwer, founder of OM, was only for one year. He began tucked in a corner answering letters. As Verwer said, "Jonathan planned to help with OM for a year but stayed for a lifetime."

Of his early days with OM, Jonathan said he was "the brakes of the movement" whereas Verwer was "the motor." He was skeptical of the ministry's need to reach out to teens since so many other organizations were doing so, and he questioned the wisdom of purchasing an oceangoing ship. However, he witnessed how God used the ship and OM's outreach and was thankful "God uses weak people to accomplish His purposes."

In 1982 Jonathan was in a serious car accident that might have changed the course of his life. However, God had him exactly where he was supposed to be. He remained with Operation Mobilization. Because of his injuries, he became a paraplegic, and he spent the next 30 years ministering from a wheelchair. Though he faced many obstacles, he also saw the benefits of his disability. "People don't need pity, but they do need empathy. Sometimes God uses distress to make us more understanding of other people."

Jonathan knew the challenges of living with a disability but didn't let it stop him. He continued to travel all around Europe, and in the early 90s he became a founding member of the European Disability Network. Jonathan will be missed, yet his faithful legacy will live on.

"We could use your expertise. Would you consider helping us, Deb?"

"When have I ever turned down a challenge?" Anyone who knew me well knew the answer to that question.

I agreed to be on the committee for the 2001 Summer Games that were held in London, Ontario. My perspective as a former athlete, a boccia referee and someone who faced the challenges of being in a wheelchair was invaluable. It took two full years to plan and prepare for the Games.

"We can't put the athletes in that hotel," I said.

"Why?"

"They have very limited wheelchair accessibility."

"Oh, I see what you mean."

"How about this venue, Deb? Is it doable?"

"Not really."

I not only helped select hotels and venues for the Games, I taught volunteers what to say to the visiting athletes—and what not to say. I taught them how to help athletes disembark the planes and get settled into their accommodations.

As always, my parents were supportive of my efforts. I enjoyed sharing our progress with them.

"Isn't it great, Dad? All the athletes will be competing at the same time, those who are disabled and those who aren't."

"It's about time," my dad said.

"It sure is."

I'd waited for that day for many years, and I was thrilled to be part of the committee that helped bring about the change.

The swimming events were held the first week at the London Aquatic Centre, and the track events were held the second week, most at the University of Western Ontario. There was lots to do.

"You look tired. Do you really have to be at the Games every day?"

"There's always something that needs my attention." I did get to go home at midday, but then it was back again in each evening.

"Deb, you've got another call," Sylvia said.

"Seriously? If that stupid phone rings one more time..."

I never did like cellphones. I had to listen to the caller and then explain the answer to my helper, who would, in turn, relay it to the person on the other end of the line. What a bother! Well, it was sort of a bother, but I was actually delighted to help. So many others had done so to make it possible for me to compete.

The whole process was exhausting. My body pretty much shut down at the closing ceremonies, but my responsibilities weren't over. Wrap-up meetings. Some minor issues. Training those who would organize the next Games. From the beginning, being on the committee had given me the opportunity to exercise my organizational abilities, but it was definitely a challenge.

Fun with 2011 Canada Games Mascot, Wagush

CHAPTER ELEVEN

Foray into the Business World

Having CP has given me a unique understanding of many needs that go unnoticed by the able-bodied world.

"Mom, Dad, I want to start my own business."

"Doing what?" Mom asked.

"Selling wheelchairs."

The narrow wheel base and limited turning radius of the British chair made it perfect not only for sports, but also for living in cramped quarters. It did not, however, have all of the features many people needed. For example, the seat did not recline electronically, and the leg rests had to be raised manually.

"Would you be willing to recommend this wheelchair to your clients?" I asked the therapist sitting across from me in his office.

"It looks like a good option," he said, looking over the promotional materials. "I'm sure we could work something out."

Although they never suggested it in so many words, the implication was evident. I was not willing to give kickbacks, so this made things difficult, this plus the fact that the chairs had to be tested and approved for sale in Ontario, which they eventually were.

"It's great, Deb. I think you'll like it," my business partner said.

"Is it big enough?"

"Yeah, we can use it as our warehouse and our showroom. There's even enough room for you to have an office."

Ben had found a building on Wonderland Road that seemed perfect for our needs. However, there were drawbacks with this location. One night I sat in the living room discussing them with my parents.

"It's certainly big enough," I said.

"That's good," my dad said.

"But one of the problems is that it's outside the city limits."

"No Paratransit?" Mom asked.

"Nope. I suppose I should look into buying a van."

"We can drive you back and forth," Dad said.

"Thanks. I appreciate that." My parents often took me where I needed to go, but they travelled to Florida regularly, and I wasn't about to hold them back from enjoying my dad's retirement. Eventually, I hired a driver.

We imported not only wheelchairs but sports equipment as well. The most popular were the boccia sets that were made in Britain and Denmark. I sold our goods at the store and at trade shows. I travelled across Ontario and also to Penticton, British Columbia.

Joni and Friends held a show in Knoxville, Tennessee, in 1994. My dad, one of my friends, my attendant and I headed south. We were gone only three days. What a whirlwind trip! While I didn't sell any wheelchairs, I did get my name out there.

The trips were tiring but part of being in business.

Ben looked disappointed, but he nodded. "That makes sense."

We sat quietly while Ben absorbed the news. Then he said, "I know you wanted to expand so you could hire some staff members with disabilities."

"I know, but we can only do what we can do."

The business never took off the way I'd hoped, but the two or three co-op students grew more confident in the six short weeks they were with us, and I was never one to underestimate the importance of helping just one person.

Selling goal balls and boccia sets brought in enough money to keep the business afloat. However, we only sold one wheelchair per year, and eventually I had to stop trying. The company graciously took back the unsold chairs and cancelled our outstanding debt.

"Ben," I said one day after we'd stopped selling the chairs, "I think it's best if I move the business back home. This..." I gestured to the warehouse and showroom, "it's just too much."

He nodded.

My dad built a floor over the indoor swimming pool, and I set up shop at home. I no longer needed a ride to work. If I was tired or not feeling well, I could go to my room and rest. And, of course, I saved a lot of money without the overhead of maintaining a building.

In 1998 we drove to a boccia meet in New York. The organizers rented 30 sets for the competition and then decided to purchase them after the meet. It made the trip worthwhile. In fact, travelling was one of my favourite parts of being in business.

Even so, as time went on, it became more and more difficult to make ends meet. With the advent of Internet sales, people could buy online and pay wholesale prices. I could not compete with that. It became evident it was time to close up shop. The business ran from 1990 to 2000. In no way do I consider the venture a failure. I was able to use the business skills I'd learned in school. I was able to travel and meet many wonderful people. It was exciting to be an entrepreneur for a time. It wasn't all I'd hoped, but I'd learned to accept change.

Running my own business opened many exciting opportunities, including attending the People in Motion trade show, Canada's premier event for people with disabilities, seniors with special needs and professionals working in related areas. The show was held annually. My mom, and sometimes my dad, would accompany me. The show was where I first saw information about service dogs raised in Oakville. I'd always wanted one, so with an application in hand, the possibility of getting my own service dog was so close I could taste it. It has been exciting to see how everything is my life has been intertwined.

Wheelchair chin control made by Debbie's dad

CHAPTER TWELVE

Lego, Another Name for Independence

"Oh, Mommy, look at the dog. Can I pet him?'

"My Buster was my best friend for ten years."

"Oh, cool. I have a dog too."

All of a sudden it didn't matter that I was in a wheelchair, that my body jerked or that my speech was sometimes difficult to understand. I was a fellow pet owner, and that was all that mattered.

One sunny afternoon in June of 1993, Lego, a two-year-old standard poodle, came bounding into my home and into my heart.

"We've done the first phase of Lego's training," said Jac, one of the two trainers from the Oakville Lions Foundation. "Now it's time to teach the two of you to work together."

I had been waiting years for that day. When I was especially excited it was even more difficult to control my limbs. I had to take several deep breaths to calm my racing heart.

"This is how to get Lego ready to go for a walk. Getting the collar over his head will take some practice, but you'll learn to do it."

The trainers would show me what to do and then leave us alone for a few hours.

"OK, Buddy, if you're patient with me, I promise to be patient with you."

Deb, you can do this.

Lego's abilities began to grow, and my limitations began to fall away.

"You're doing great, Deb. We have to leave now."

I looked from the trainers to Lego and back again.

"You really think I'm ready?"

Diane, the second trainer, put her hand on my shoulder and smiled.

"Remember," Jac said, "we'll be back to visit, and you can call for help anytime."

The door closed and I heard the car drive away. I looked over at my new companion.

"This is *our* home now, boy."

And didn't he know it? It wasn't long before he'd laid claim to the couch. But as soon as he heard me switch on my power chair he was by my side, ready for action. Lego wasn't simply my pet; he was my freedom. Without him, I couldn't live on my own. He picked up the things I dropped, opened doors and acted as my personal bodyguard.

"Time to hit up the mall, boy. Come."

Lego pranced over to my side.

"Good boy."

I slipped the collar over his head. In the process, my wallet slipped off my lap.

"Fetch."

Nothing.

"Lego, fetch."

He picked up the wallet and laid it on my lap.

"Good dog."

We started for the door.

"I guess I shouldn't leave the light on. Lego, up. Push. That's it. Down."

The day-to-day things so many people take for granted had caused me so much frustration. After I got my dog, things began to change.

"That will be $25.50," the saleswoman said.

"Lego, take." He took the wallet from my lap.

"Up. Give," I said.

"You better make the right change," one of the woman's co-workers said, "or her dog just might take matters into his own paws."

We laughed.

"Lego, take. Good boy. Down. Give."

My wallet was back on my lap, and we were off to the next store. Lego accompanied me to the movies, church, anywhere I went. He even flew with me, sometimes getting better service than I did. There were other times I had to educate the public.

"You can't bring that dog in here."

"Yes, I can."

"We have a no-pets-allowed policy."

"Lego's not a pet. He's a certified service dog."

"Oh *really?*"

"He's in harness. I always keep him with me. And I have a card with his picture on it to prove that he has been through training."

"Oh..."

Sometimes a conversation was sufficient. At other times I was forced to write a letter explaining what a service dog did and why I needed him with me. Although it has never happened to me, I know of situations in which the police were called. It is actually illegal not to allow service dogs and their owners access to public services, such as train and boat rides.

When it was time for bed, Lego would turn off the light and close my door. As part of his training, I gave him a treat when he did this. And that dog lived to eat!

One morning at 2:00 a.m., I awoke to a bright light in my eyes. Lego was standing by the light switch, wagging his tail, eager for his "reward." His chocolate-brown eyes melted my heart.

"Seriously, how can I be mad at you? Tomorrow do you think you could at least wait until the sun comes up?"

I instructed him to turn off the light and drifted back to sleep.

Lego's head was at the perfect height to snatch a bun—or whatever was sitting on the table—without being noticed. Sometimes what he stole didn't agree with him. One day after he ate something that made him sick, I became frustrated.

"Lego, if you love me, why do you do this?"

That question haunted me. I did plenty of things that weren't good for me, and I wondered if God felt the same way. Was He challenging me to be less stubborn and do what He asked of me?

I learned many lessons from my years with Lego. I will never have children, but like everyone, I need to be needed. While my dog looked after me in many ways, I also looked after him. I fed him, took him to the vet, and kept his coat and nails trimmed—among many other things. We spent many years together in a wonderful give-and-take relationship.

As old age crept up on my treasured companion, he seemed to cling to me. He needed my help more than ever. His hearing eventually failed, and he lost interest in food. Even then, Lego knew when I was sick or feeling down. He would stay by my side or climb up on my bed.

On our last night together, Lego's back legs gave out, and he dragged himself on his belly to be close to me. I looked into his eyes and knew our time as a team had come to an end. I took him to the clinic, where he collapsed again. The staff tried to make him comfortable.

"Deb, we're very sorry..."

The tears poured from my eyes and I nodded. It was time for him to go. Lego looked so peaceful that it seemed he would get up any minute. But I knew he was really gone when my wheelchair motor clicked and he remained motionless.

When I think about Lego, my eyes still mist over. I'll always cherish our years together. After that, Tate was my service dog for over eight years, and now Maple fills the role. It's hard to get so attached only to say goodbye, but I would never want to be without these wonderful friends, my source of independence.

Debbie and her first service dog, Lego

CHAPTER THIRTEEN

Help Wanted

A new day dawns and daylight trickles into my room. I open my eyes and yawn. What will the day bring? Will someone need a smile of encouragement? Or maybe a kind word? Then I remember I would have to stay right where I am if it weren't for the amazing people in my life.

First it was my parents. When I was young, they did everything for me—everything I couldn't do for myself. My mom made sure I woke up on time. She took me to the washroom and bathed me. Then she got me dressed. My dad did the more physically demanding tasks, like carrying me where I needed to go—and coming up behind me and tipping my chair back when I was least expecting it. That was one of the ways he assured me I was just like everyone else—and one of the ways he scared me silly.

"One day you'll need other people to help you," my mom said.

"No way!"

I couldn't imagine anyone else helping with my personal care. It was unthinkable, but the time did come. Of course no one would love me and give me the same tender care as my parents, but over the years, hundreds of people have helped me in various capacities. Some of my mom's friends helped when she was away. Mom always made sure they knew exactly what to do. But eventually, occasional help was not enough.

"I've been hired as a computer programmer," I said to my dad.

"That's great. Where?"

"The Children's Centre. It will be so good to go back and work with the kids. I learned so much from my years at the centre. Now I can give something back."

"You're going to need help."

"Yeah, I know."

I hired an assistant with my own money, and that worked for a while. But after that first summer, most of the money I earned went to pay my assistant. I needed help to cover my staff's wages, so I applied to an organization called Cheshire London.

"I've been accepted," I said to my mom one day after I read my mail.

"To the outreach program?"

"Yeah."

People travelled from home to home, helping where needed. As grateful as I was, the program had limitations. Workers came only at scheduled times. There was absolutely no flexibility. In the beginning, I only had help for one hour each morning. When my parents travelled, that was definitely not enough.

"Tracy, I really appreciate the help, but I'm not going to need you for a couple of weeks."

"Deb, you need to know if someone doesn't come, they'll drop you from the program."

"Seriously? Even if I don't need the help for two weeks?"

"'Afraid so. They will hold your spot for seven days. That's it."

Tracy wasn't my only helper in the early days. I had to accept whomever they sent. It's not easy to entrust total strangers with my personal care. Some came only once, giving me no time to develop any kind of relationship with them.

As time went on, my helpers were available for longer periods of time. However, it was not enough, especially when my parents were away. At most, I had someone with me for an hour and a half morning and night Monday through Friday and only two hours total Saturday and Sunday. I had to rely on family and friends to help with things like going to the washroom and preparing meals.

Although I felt vulnerable and trapped in my own home, I was with the outreach program for about eight years. That would change in 1995. The Ontario government began a direct funding program.

"So, did you send them everything they need to go over before your interview tomorrow?" my dad asked.

"I sent what they asked for with my application, including a budget and a list of my needs."

"That's good. I hope it all comes together for you, Deb."

"Me too."

It was a lengthy interview, and all I could do after it was over was go home and wait to hear. I was nervous that I wouldn't be accepted, but in April of 1995 I got word that I qualified. I was one of approximately 80 people who were chosen to participate in the pilot project. I felt as if I'd been released from bondage.

"So exactly how does the program work?" Mom asked.

"The government allocates funds, and I use them to hire my own staff."

"That will be such a blessing," my dad said.

"Yeah. And you know what?"

"What?" he asked.

"I've noticed I've been getting fewer migraines."

"How come?" my mom asked.

"I think it's because so much of the stress has been relieved."

"Makes sense," Dad said.

After being accepted into the program, I had to prepare a job description, advertise for staff and interview those who applied. My background in accounting came in helpful. I set up all the bookwork and did the accounting. I kept a separate bank account and paid my staff directly. I even had the opportunity to help others in the program with their bookkeeping.

Things came together quickly for me. By May of the same year, my staff of four or five was in place. I got to train each attendant myself, and that made all the difference. Cathy was even able to attend the '96 Paralympics in Atlanta with me.

"I feel like a teenager again, but this time it's even better," I said to a friend over coffee.

"How come?" she asked.

"I've got more freedom than ever...and more control over my life."

My whole life changed. My handpicked attendants came to my home. They helped with my personal care and worked in my kitchen. They took me shopping and to my various appointments. Their help allowed me to be involved in the lives of my nieces and nephews (I just love being an aunt!), to have specially trained care while I was in the hospital recovering from surgery and to attend Dan and Grace's wedding in Belgium.

The direct funding program is so much more flexible than the outreach program was—for me and for my staff. I have the freedom to hire attendants for a predetermined number of hours per month, but what hours I require help is up to me. If someone is unavailable, another attendant covers for her.

Even now that I live in Huntsville there are a few staff members from London who come up for a weekend—and sometimes a whole week—when they need a break from the city or when a local attendant needs to get away. That's dedication far beyond that of an ordinary employee.

"Another headache?" my attendant asked when she arrived.

"Yep." My voice was barely audible.

"Let me take the dog out. Then I'll be back to get you ready for the day."

"OK. Thanks."

My staff members learn my routine, my moods, my ups and downs, even the illnesses I have to deal with from time to time. It's critical that I hire attendants who are dependable and who like what they're doing. After all, if my attendant doesn't show up, I could be stuck in bed all day.

My family has always been very important to me. I can never express sufficient gratitude to my parents for all they've done over the years. I moved to Huntsville in 2004 to be close to them and other members of my family. If it hadn't been for my staff here, it wouldn't have been possible. I would likely have been stuck in an apartment in London—where there are more potential staff members to choose from. I'm sure I wouldn't have enjoyed that.

Some of my attendants have become good friends. It has not, however, always been easy. Not all the people I hire turn out to be a good fit. My least favourite part of the process is firing an attendant. Thankfully, over the years I've learned what to look for, what questions to ask and what qualities I need in my staff members. I rarely have to let any of them go.

It turns out Mom was right. I did need others to help, and God has always provided.

CHAPTER FOURTEEN

Go North, Young Woman

"It's a nice place to visit, but I really don't want to live there."

That's how I felt about moving to Huntsville. I enjoyed going to the cottage—in the good weather. My life, however, was in London. I worked in London, was involved in sports in London, went to church in London and sat on several committees in London.

"Deb," my dad said, "we're thinking of selling the house and moving to Huntsville."

My body jerked and my head snapped to look in his direction. "You're kidding, right?"

Dad shook his head. "Nope."

"What am I going to do?"

"We want you to come with us," my mom said.

"And leave London?"

"It won't be that bad," Dad said.

"Remember that one winter?"

"Which one?" Mom asked.

"The one when we couldn't get the car up the driveway."

"And we had to pull you on the toboggan?" my mom said.

"That was fun, wasn't it?" Dad asked.

I rolled my eyes. "Not the way I remember it. It took an hour to get to the house, and all three of us were frozen, tired and grumpy. I don't want to live in the Land of Snow."

It wasn't just the winters that made me hesitant to move. I'd gotten used to my freedom in the city. Huntsville was a much smaller community, and it didn't have businesses geared toward those with disabilities. There were no colleges or universities nearby—which was where I found many of my staff members. And accessibility was always an issue.

"So where would I live?" I asked.

"In the house with us," my dad said. "We'll get it all set up."

I stared at him for a moment. "But it will be hard for my staff to get there, and you'll be in Florida for the winter."

"It will be okay."

A short time later, my brother Dan made a proposal.

"Deb, what would you think of living in your own place?"

"Huh? How's that possible?"

"Grace and I are building."

"Uh-huh. And?"

"We'd like to build an attached apartment so you can be close to us and the kids."

"Are you serious?"

"When haven't I been...OK, scratch that. But yes. Then you could live on the main road. Plus, we'd like you to help with the planning."

And I did—everything from the layout to the paint colours to the carpets. *Maybe it's going to be all right.*

"So what do you think, Tate?" I asked my service dog. "Would you like to have room to run?"

He wagged his tail and looked into my eyes as if he knew what I was asking.

I contacted several people up north to see what kinds of services were available and what kind of wheelchair accessibility there was. Thankfully, the year before I moved, they opened a Walmart and a bigger, more accessible grocery store I could shop in. But the need for staff was always in the back of my mind.

It turned out all that was about to fall into place too. I was helping at a boccia tournament in London in February 2004. I was doing my best to get my friend Anna an interview with representatives from a London group home. I told her if I wasn't moving, I'd hire her myself. That night I received a phone call.

"So, did you mean it?" Anna asked.

"Mean what?"

"What you said about hiring me."

"Well, yeah, but..."

"I'm serious."

"Anna, your life is here. Huntsville is very different from London—very different."

"I really think this is the right thing to do."

"If you're sure, we can set up an interview."

I got off the phone and shook my head. It had taken me three years to decide to move north, and Anna had decided in as many hours.

I was going up in March to take some of my things. Anna went with me to look around.

This will convince her to stay where she is. But no, I was wrong. After our trip, she was even more determined than ever. It was convenient that she could train in London. Gradually, my other staff members took other jobs or moved away. Everything was coming together.

Moving day arrived: June 29, 2004. I thought I would be sad and weepy, but the day turned out to be a lot of fun. Friends came to help me pack. It was like a party—even though the water main on my street broke. Oh, well. My friends brought bottled water, and we made do.

"Your sister's here."

"Hi, Deb," Sharon said. "Everything ready to go?"

"Yep."

My friends loaded the moving van, and Sharon headed north. She had to have the van back to the rental place by midnight. She was very tired by the end of the day. And so was I by the time my friend Sylvia got me to Listowel, where we spent the night with another friend, Cathy.

By the time Sylvia and I arrived in Huntsville the next day, my mom was wondering if I'd changed my mind. Sylvia stayed for two weeks and helped me get settled. Other friends pitched in too and were an amazing help.

"What is it, Deb?" Sylvia asked the day before she was to head back to London.

My voice caught, and I was hardly able to answer. I was one big teardrop. I cried and cried and cried. Although I would visit from time to time, my years in London were officially a thing of the past.

"So Deb, we're heading to the city to pack up our things," Mom said three weeks after I'd moved in.

They had a lifetime's worth of stuff to pack. It was an adventure, but not the only one. When the moving truck got to Huntsville, it missed the turnoff and ended up in the ditch. Dan had to get a tractor to pull it out.

It was a cool, wet summer, and I didn't mind staying indoors. Dan and Dad had built my apartment first, but it was still a work in progress. Dan and Grace were staying offsite while they built their home. It was not easy to get around, even in my power chair—everything was built on a hill—but I managed.

When I learned Huntsville would be hosting the 2006 Paralympic Games, I volunteered for the committee and soon met many great people from town. During the process, I learned much about my new town. Being involved was a good way to begin to feel like part of the community. After the Games, I joined the town's accessibility committee.

There are times I still hit the road for a shopping trip. There's nothing like shopping in London. It has everything I could possibly want. Sometimes I go to Barrie or North Bay, which are still bigger centres than Huntsville. There isn't much choice when it comes to clothing in our little town. I can't have my power chair serviced the same day, and that's inconvenient. However, things have greatly improved over the years.

"Aunt Deb, we have another snow day."

"Cool. What do you want to do?"

Ninety percent of the kids are bused to school in the area, so they get a lot of vacation days during the winter.

There are a lot of trees and hydro lines. When there is a big storm, which happens often, the hydro can be out for days. No heat. No stove. No water. (We need electricity to pump the water.)

"The generator's on."

"Quick, fill up the water jugs...and please, please, please flush the toilet."

We have storms in the winter, black flies in the spring and an influx of vacationers in the summer. We live near a campground, so we are very aware when the camping season is in full swing.

My favourite time of year is the fall. The leaves are spectacular. It isn't too cold. And everything is peaceful. Plus, it's easy for me to get around.

It took some convincing, but I learned a lot about God when I finally agreed to move north. I saw how unwaveringly dependable He is and how He provides for all my needs. There are many people in Ontario these days who can't find a doctor. I had one even before I moved. I have a vehicle that makes it easy for me to get around, and I have a beautiful home. I'm involved in a wonderful church and have spoken at the schools in the area.

Because I live in Huntsville, I have the privilege of spending time with my brother's four children and my sister's three. Being part of their lives is very special to me. I try to be a fun aunt.

"Can you come to my soccer game?"

"Sure I can."

"How about my school play?"

"I wouldn't miss it."

"Is it OK if I sleep over, Aunt Deb?"

"You bet."

"Can we come for movie night?"

"For sure."

"Will there be candy?"

"Of course; just don't tell your mom."

I laugh. The kids know I try to honour their mom's wishes, but it's nice to have our running jokes just the same.

It would take a lot to get me to move back to London. I have everything I need: great staff, although each has her unique quirks (we laugh a lot), and my family. The change was hard, but change often is. It stretched me and helped me grow closer to God, and that's my ultimate goal in life.

I do miss the city from time to time. I miss my friends and the conveniences. However, I do not miss the traffic and the busyness. Huntsville is laid back and easygoing. Although I don't always know exactly why I'm here, I seek to make the most of every day. There are times when I get down. When I do, I listen to praise music. It lifts my spirits. The move north has been worth it.

That's the way it is with God. I had to trust Him with His plans for my life...and I'm glad I did.

Debbie resumes painting after moving to Huntsville

A Note from the Author

My prayer for you, dear reader, is that you will know without a doubt that you are loved by Almighty God and that He has a special plan for your life.

When I was a child I didn't want to lead a boring life. I didn't want to be unemployed when I grew up. I didn't want to be stuck at home all day. And I didn't want to remain single.

So, what happened?

God changed me.

I work from home—and love it.

I'm single, but I don't feel alone.

And sometimes I pray for a boring day so I can rest.

My goal after high school was to get a job so I wouldn't have to rely on a government pension. Finding work is difficult enough, but add to it a disability, and potential employers only see what you can't do, not what you can. When the jobs I did get didn't work out, I tried starting my own business, but I only made enough to pay my bills and my staff.

Working from home is much more enjoyable. It doesn't involve the same level of stress. If I worked outside the home, I would face many challenges. I can't drive, so I would constantly have to arrange a ride. I would have to factor in sickness, bad weather and people being late. Plus, if I got a migraine, I couldn't rest. When I did work away from home, it usually took two hours to get to and from work. That was frustrating and such a huge waste of time. It is so much easier working at my computer in my home office.

I had hoped to marry and have children, but God had other plans. I did date a few guys over the years. One relationship ended so painfully I contemplated ending my life, but God showed me He had other things for me to do. People come and people go, but God has been my constant, and

I know I will never be alone. He showed me that life is about serving Him. Jesus is my bridegroom, and one day I will dance with Him.

My sister and brothers married, and their spouses have been good to me. Between them, I have ten nieces and nephews. I have the privilege of helping them with homework, feeding them sugar and sending them home. They come for sleepovers, and we do many other fun things together. I've helped coach Ainsley's ball hockey team at church. They even borrow my spare wheelchair when they break a leg or a foot. It gives me great joy to be with them.

One of the keys to joy is to focus on the positives and keep your eyes on Jesus.

When I was younger, people suggested I would be a good prayer warrior. At that time, the idea didn't thrill me. But the closer I've grown to Christ, the more of a privilege I find it to meet with and talk to Him. I see answers to prayer every day.

Meeting The Honourable David C. Onley in 2008

About the Authors

Deb Willows is a writer, speaker, former Paralympic athlete and boccia coach, inductee into the Canadian Cerebral Palsy Sports Hall of Fame, former business owner, bookkeeper, daughter, sister, aunt and friend.

Deb has lived a remarkable life to date. She wants to share her experiences and insights with readers and does so in a conversational, approachable style. She has written several articles, travelled extensively and spoken in many venues. Deb's work appeared in the books *Heal Our Land* and *Everyday Grace, Everyday Miracles*. She wrote an article that was published in *Faith and Friends*. Deb has been the keynote speaker at banquets, graduations, church events, detention centres, retreats and school assemblies.

Her heart's cry is to let people know that the fulfillment of dreams takes hard work, the encouragement of family and friends and the grace of God. Deb has been doing this for years and believes, through her book, she can continue.

There have been many naysayers claiming Deb would never be able to accomplish much of anything, but she has proven them wrong and set an example for all who have hopes and dreams—and obstacles to overcome. This book will be simply one more accomplishment proving she is "living beyond her circumstances."

Steph Beth Nickel is a freelance writer and editor. She is part of the Christian Editing Services team, an online business providing various services to writers. Among her many editing projects, she served as first editor of R. H. Delion's novel *Justified*. Her book review of M. D. Meyer's novel *Joshua* was used in its entirety as a foreword for the book. Steph also blogs about her diverse interests at Steph Nickel's Eclectic Interests, shares weekly writing prompts at Christian Editing Service's Monday Motivation, and is a regular guest blogger for Kimberley Payne.

Steph is a certified personal trainer and thereby is interested in the athletic aspect of Deb's story. More importantly, she is adamant that the world needs to learn about the Paralympics and the courage and strength of the athletes—and all of those who live full lives despite their physical challenges. She was amazed when she saw the athletes and coaches honoured at the Canadian Cerebral Palsy Sports Hall of Fame dinner and for the first time realized just what remarkable athletes they are.

Steph is a member of The Word Guild, contributes five times per week to their Facebook page, is first editor of *Write! On*, The Word Guild's biweekly news bulletin for members, and volunteers for the annual Write! Canada conference. Steph is also a new member of InScribe Christian Writers' Fellowship.

Steph believes relationships are what life is all about. She is thankful for the friendship that has developed between Deb and herself. During the time they have spent working on the book, Steph has gained insights that have helped her not only co-write *Living Beyond My Circumstances* but also appreciate Deb's day-to-day life. She considers her own life richer because of it.

Twenty years of medals

APPENDIX 1

Author's Biography

Deb Willows was born in 1961. When she failed to hit the markers of normal childhood development, doctors discovered she had been born with CP, a neurological condition that affects motor control. Doctors advised her parents, Dan and Marg Willows, to put her in an institution, believing untrained parents were unable to meet the special needs of children with CP. They would hear nothing of it.

The Willows never referred to their daughter as disabled. (And that was long before it was politically incorrect to do so.) Deb's younger brothers, Danny and Terry, and her younger sister, Sharon, grew up seeing their sister as normal. They treated her as they would any other big sister. The entire family was ahead of its time.

Many parents squelch their children's dreams and aspirations, believing their children must learn to live "in the real world." While Deb's parents accepted there would be unique challenges along the way, they expected the same of their firstborn as they did of all their children: do your best, dream big dreams and work hard to accomplish them.

And the result? Graduation with honours—and a business certificate—from Saunders Secondary School, the school for able-bodied students that opened its doors because Deb wanted to attend "real school."

And those dreams? Deb travelled the world representing Canada, first as an athlete, then as the first ever disabled boccia referee. ("Disabled" is a term she uses to refer to herself. However, it is obviously not a term that held her back.) And how did her parents help her realize her dreams? Well, for one thing, they built an indoor pool in their home so she could practice. Now, that's commitment!

Deb has won countless medals and set many world records. She has blazed the trail for other disabled people and their families in many areas:

education, sports, business, direct funding for hiring and training staff, living independently with the support of family and the aid of her service dog, speaking, writing and so much more.

And what's most important to this amazing woman who has spent half a century *living beyond her circumstances*? "When I introduce someone to Jesus Christ, now that's pure gold."

If you would like to contact Deb, you are invited to visit her website, www.deborahwillows.com.

Inducted into CCPSA Hall of Fame, 2007

APPENDIX 2

Highlights of Author's Athletic Timeline

1981–1983	Regionals and Provincials
1984	Paralympic Games in New York
1985	U.S. National Cerebral Palsy Games
1986	International Games in Belgium
1987	Awarded Athlete of the Year
1987	Can-Am Games in New York
1987	Won Triathlon in Ottawa
1988	Paralympic Games in Seoul, Korea
1989	Awarded Female Swimmer of the Year
1989	World Games in Nottingham, England
1989	Took Boccia Refereeing Course in Portugal
1989	Trained Boccia Referees for all meets in Ontario, Canada
1990	World Games in Assen, Holland
1990–1991	Coached Canadian Boccia Team in Portugal
	Organized Boccia Refereeing Course in Toronto, Ontario
	Served as Member of International Boccia Committee
1992	Refereed Boccia at Paralympics in Barcelona, Spain
1993	Refereed for World Competitions in England and Belgium

1994	Refereed for World Championships in Sheffield, England
1995	Inducted into the Hall of Fame for Ontario Cerebral Palsy Sports
1996	Refereed for the Paralympic Games in Atlanta, Georgia
1998	Head Referee at Nationals
1998–2001	Integration Advisor for 2001 Canada Games
1999	Head Referee at Nationals
2003	Queen Elizabeth II Golden Jubilee Medal (2002)
2007	Inducted into the Canadian Cerebral Palsy Sports Hall of Fame http://www.ccpsa.ca/en/aboutus/hof/hofinductees.aspx

Receiving Queen's Medal—what an honour!

APPENDIX 3

The Romans Road to Salvation

These are the steps along the Romans Road that lead to salvation and eternal life.

Realize we are all sinners who can never be good enough to earn our way to heaven. (Romans 3:23 says, *"For all have sinned and fall short of the glory of God."*)

Acknowledge that eternal separation from God is the outcome of this sin and realize the gift of eternal life comes through Jesus Christ. (Romans 6:23 says, *"For the wages of sin is death, but the gift of God is eternal life in Christ Jesus our Lord."*)

Accept that this gift is available because Jesus died for us, paying the debt we could never pay. (Romans 5:8 says, *"But God demonstrates his own love for us in this: While we were still sinners, Christ died for us."*)

The next step is twofold. We must confess that Jesus is Lord, and we must believe that God raised Him from the dead. If we proclaim with our mouth and believe in our heart, we will be saved. (Romans 10:9 says, *"If you declare with your mouth, 'Jesus is Lord,' and believe in your heart that God raised him from the dead, you will be saved."*)

After we've taken step 4, we can rest secure, knowing we have been "justified [made right with God] through faith." We can experience true "peace with God." (Romans 5:1 says, *"Therefore, since we have been justified through faith, we have peace with God through our Lord Jesus Christ."*)

Deb travelled this road when she was a girl. Her parents took her to church from the time she was a newborn. When she was seven, Pastor Roy Lawson gave a message on how to know if you are going to heaven. Later, in bed by herself, Deb asked Jesus to forgive her sins and come into her life. That very night, she become convinced that God had a purpose for allowing her to have CP. She didn't have a clue what it was, but she knew she could trust Him.

When she told her mom the next morning, Deb didn't expect the response she received. "Why didn't you ask us to help you with that?" Being independent, she wondered why her mom would ask. It wasn't until she was an adult that she came to understand the joy of hearing someone else—especially a family member—ask Jesus into his or her life.

At 13 Deb was baptized in accordance with the Scriptures. Her dad carried her to the change room, then left to put on his swim trunks and robe. He got into the baptismal tank, and her mom handed Deb to him. He then carried her to the pastor who performed the service.

When she was 20, Deb rededicated her life to Christ at a Barry Moore meeting that was held at her church. Although the Lord promised never to leave or forsake us, recommitting our lives to Him is a good reminder for us and a good testimony to others.

Many believers have a particular verse that means a lot to them. They call it a "life verse." Deb's is Philippians 4:13, which says, "*I can do all things through Christ who strengthens me*" (NKJV).

Though she has accomplished many incredible things in the course of her life, honouring and glorifying Him are her number-one priority, and it all started when she recognized that God had a special plan for her life. If you would like to discuss it with her, please contact her through her website, www.deborahwillows.com.

APPENDIX 4

The Paralympic Games

Too many people know nothing of these amazing athletes and these amazing Games. Of course, the Olympics are remarkable evidence of what men and women are capable of, but you would think, with all the hype, that when they're over, it's all wrapped up for another four years. That isn't the case. After the Olympics, the Paralympics get into full swing. More world-class events. More world-class athletes. Records broken...and some hearts.

It all began back in 1948 when Sir Ludwig Guttman arranged a competition for WWII veterans with spinal cord injuries, and it went from there. The first Olympic-style games for disabled athletes were held in Rome in 1960. The first Paralympic Winter Games were held in Sweden in 1976.

Four hundred athletes from 23 countries participated in 1960. In 2008 that number had grown to 3,951 athletes from 146 countries. The 2008 Games were held in Beijing. The athletes first began to compete at the same venues as the Olympics in 1988. In 1992 the Winter Games were first held at the same venues. Just one more way to affirm the class of athletes the Paralympians truly are. From 2012 on, the applicants for future host cities have had to agree to host the Paralympics as well.

The 2012 Games were held in London, England. The 2014 Winter Games will be held Sochi, Russia, and the 2016 Games in Rio de Janeiro.

The Paralympic Principles give fans a glimpse of what the Games are all about. They include quality, elite, exciting, inspirational, fair play, quantity, viable, sustainable/dynamic, universality, equitable, global and balance.

Athletes compete in events such as boccia ball, cross country skiing, ice sledge hockey, powerlifting, shooting and swimming.

As stated on the official Paralympic website (www.paralympic.org), "The purpose of London 2012 is to deliver accessible and inclusive designs for all facilities, maximize media coverage and strengthen the Paralympic Movement. The Olympic and Paralympic Games are the pinnacle of every athlete's career. London 2012 will strive to provide conditions that enable the athletes to compete in an environment of excellence, friendship and enjoyment."

The site goes on to say of the Winter Games, "The aim of Sochi 2014 is to stage unique Paralympic Winter Games and further strengthen and promote the Paralympic Movement by providing excellent conditions for athletes to compete, delivering a high level of accessibility and maximizing media coverage."

In my opinion, the media coverage in particular has been sadly lacking. It wasn't until I (Steph Nickel) began working on this book with Deb that I had any more than a vague knowledge of the Paralympic Games. Sadly, I wasn't even aware that the Games took place the same year—and at the same venues—as the Olympic Games. Every major television network carries coverage of the Olympic Games. Few carry any coverage of the Paralympics. I believe it is long past time for that to change. I was thrilled to read that the purpose of the upcoming Games is to "maximize media coverage." It is my hope—it is my prayer—that they will be successful, that advertisers and sponsors will step up, and that the worldwide audience will catch Paralympic Fever.

APPENDIX 5

Resource List

The Paralympic Games - www.paralympic.ca

The Ontario Cerebral Palsy Sports Association - www.ocpsa.com

The Centre for Independent Living in Toronto - www.cilt.ca

Ministry Associations - www.billygraham.org

www.annegrahamlotz.com

www.joniandfriends.org

www.lifewithoutlimbs.org

Magazine - www.abilities.ca

Service Dogs - www.goadogs.ca

www.dogguides.com

www.assistancedogsinternational.org

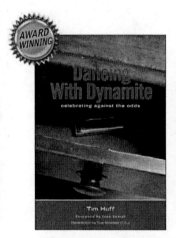
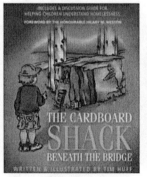